Love is the River

Learning to Live in the Flow of Divine Grace

Love is the River

Learning to Live in the Flow of Divine Grace

Ann Albers

Albers, Ann, 2006 –

Love is the River –

Learning to Live in the Flow of Divine Grace / Ann Albers

1. Mysticism 2. Spirituality I. Title

1st Printing, May 2006

4th Printing, February 2019

Paperback ISBN: 978-1-949780-00-0

eBook ISBN: 978-1-949780-88-8

Library of Congress Control Number: 2019901201

Dedication

This book is dedicated to God, who is the author of all works, and to all of the dear souls who have been part of the River's flow through my life.

Table of Contents

Acknowledgements

I am deeply grateful to so many people. Thank you, first and foremost, to my family who encouraged me to write since the first grade, and to my dear soul sisters – Deb Humphrey, Daniela Roth, Cheryl Booth, and Judith McClure – who have remained unconditionally loving throughout all my life transformations. Love and gratitude, beyond words, go to Jim Law, without whom I would not have grown into the confidence to finish this book. You are truly one of my angels.

Zeysan, thank you so much for being my soul brother and for teaching me the finer points of surrender. You are eternal friend and family. James Walker, I am blessed by your friendship and willingness to guide me into both growth and healing. Thank you also to Jessica Osborn-Turner for helping me remember the mystical universe, and to the many other teachers who have guided me along the way.

Thank you dear Summer Bacon for your friendship, your work, and your light in my life. Dr. Shawn Warwick, I am so grateful for your amazing and awesome work, and your cheerful sense of humor as well. My undying gratitude also goes to Heather Clarke for your wonderful editing skills – my books would not be readable without you!

Last but certainly not least, thank you Robin Miller, for coming into my life after I first published this book and continuing to breathe light and life into the work through your beautiful heart, music, and contributions to our live playshops. Your friendship is a beacon and inspiration in my life and continues to help me live in ever expanding flows of grace.

I can't possibly include all of my dear friends and clients who have helped contribute to my life and therefore to this book. You know who you are.

I love you all.

Ann Albers

Note from the Author

The commitment to write this book changed my life. It was as if I signed a contract with heaven saying, "I agree to give up control. I agree to allow grace to rule my life. I agree to jump into the River of Love and allow a higher power to guide my days." This became my reality.

I gave up all traditional notions of writing. No outline, no forethought, no amount of pondering the structure of my book led to any good end. In the end, I surrendered and allowed the book or rather the River to write my life. Love immediately began to make changes.

I sustained a major injury that forced me to slow down, take inventory of my activities, and settle deeply into the truth of my being. I became more authentic in my relationships. I lost a few people in my life, gained many more, and deepened old friendships. I made changes in my business to create greater balance in life and started to honor my desire for creativity. I fell deeply and truly in love with myself. As a result of allowing the River to move freely through my life and my own heart, I have been gifted with incredible joy in my life.

As you share my journey and the wisdom within these pages, you will discover gentle currents of love that come through your heart's subtle desires and intuitive stirrings. You will understand why the River of Love can hurl you into the raging rapids of chaos or the catastrophes that make you feel as if you've been tossed over a waterfall's edge. You'll discover the joy to be found in the "quiet pools" when nothing seems to be moving in your life and you'll learn to discern when to take action and "paddle downstream." You'll learn to surrender to life and free up the energy that is wasted when "fighting the River." You'll emerge from our journey with the ability and confidence to recognize the many voices, faces, and currents of grace in your life.

I recommend that you get a notebook or journal

and do the exercises in this book. There are morsels of food for thought, activities to experience, and exercises to help you embrace the currents of grace in your own life. There are no right answers, just ones that are right for you. Trust yourself.

I am honored and privileged to be your guide. Forget about the destination. There is much to be learned from the journey.

With much love,

Ann Albers

Introduction

Something moved you to pick up this book. Was it an attraction to the cover? A fascination with the title? An intuition that something within might be worthy of your time and attention? ...

... or perhaps the unseen hand of God steering you to examine and expand your capacity to love.

I believe these are all one and the same.

There is a force of Divine Love[1] that has guided you since birth. Some call this force Holy Spirit. Others have named it "prana," "chi," "life force," or "kupuri." Names don't do justice to the incredible power of this energy that courses through your life and your being.

After all, the one who moves you is God. The

---

[1] Throughout the book I will capitalize the words "Love" and "River" when I mean to imply Divine Love and the movement of Divine Love throughout your life.

motion is grace. The only motive is love.

Divine Love is the River that guides you and moves through you with every breath. Love motivates you to follow your dreams and makes you resist the things that no longer serve you. Love carries you towards unexpected circumstances that delight you and catapults you into unforeseen catastrophes that strengthen you or help you change the course of your life.

Love is the River of life in which you swim, sink, or struggle to stay afloat. Your relationship to the flow of Divine Love determines the quality of your existence.

Surrender to the River. Allow Love to guide you, and you will be carried towards an unimaginable life. The dreams of your soul will come true in miraculous fashion. The River will guide and inform all of your choices. The twists and turns of the current will lead you on a path of self-discovery. If you cooperate with the currents of Love, your days will flow more smoothly. You'll receive and heed Divine guidance. You'll leave behind useless baggage such as fear, shame, guilt, anxiety, worry, and anger. You'll find right livelihood, recreation for your soul, and a graceful balance between the two. At long last, you'll be steered towards others of like mind and heart, truly connecting with the family of your soul.

If you allow the River to guide you, you must give up a large degree of control. You cannot rush the flow. You cannot stop in the rapids or speed up through the quiet pools. You must allow life to take its own pace. You must allow God to support you. You must cultivate great faith.

The River is God's Love in motion and the currents of grace are its waters.

If you close your heart and mind to the River's presence, you will weary yourself trying to swim against its indomitable force. You cannot truly fight the flow of God's Love and grace in your life once you invite the very same. Pray for help and you will receive the assistance, but plan on letting go of control or else you will struggle until at long last Love wins. Surrender is a quality you will learn to cherish as you navigate the River. As you begin to release control over the details of your days, you will find that you are guided to live a life far better than you could have conceived on your own. Did you know that God longs for you to live an exquisitely inspired existence?

Of course, you can pretend to walk along the banks of the River, allowing grace to touch your mind but not your heart. You will be informed by wisdom, intuition and inspiration, but you'll do most of the work in your life yourself while angels stand by, wishing you would allow them to lend you a hand. You'll receive good ideas but you will have to implement them the old fashioned way – by the sweat of your brow – rather than by allowing Divine grace to gift you with the synchronicities and miracles that could eliminate struggle in your life.

Perhaps the worst fate of all is to ignore the River entirely. Grace will pass you by, beckoning you in every second of your life to surrender to a greater wisdom and take a leap of faith. You'll still have ideas but wonder why you can't seem to accomplish anything. You'll have inspirations but watch others carry them to fruition and reap the rewards. You'll feel victimized by life and others.

Life does not have to be a dance of adversity and an endless series of frustrations, anxieties, upsets, dissatisfaction, and pain. Instead, life is meant to be a blissful surrender to your own heart – supported by God, guided by angels, and flowing gracefully from one moment to the next. Once you accept your present position in the River, whatever that may be, then in the very next moment you can move with the never-ending currents of Love as they guide you to a life beyond your wildest dreams.

Divine Love is holding out a hand shouting to you, "Come! Follow your hearts. Leap with faith in each moment of your lives and I will catch you. I will carry you. I will guide you. I will hold you through tough times and uplift you. I will bring you home." Home, dear friends, is not a place, but rather a condition inside of your heart. Home is love. Love of self. Love of others. Love of life. Enlightenment is nothing more than the process of falling in love with all – not the warm fuzzy love we associate with romance, but rather a love based on respect, tolerance, wonder, and non-judgment.

Come journey with me. Take a leap of faith into your own heart. I can teach you to surrender to the River. I can guide you to open yourself to God's grace. I can share with you the peace of mind that comes from knowing that you are safe, cherished, guided and supported every moment of your life in an embracing current of God's Love.

Love is the River...

Come! Now, leap!

I. What Are These Waters?

A five-year-old girl stood peering over the railing on a concrete and metal suspension bridge. Behind her, the gentle muddy brown waters of the Potomac River gathered speed before cascading over a twenty-foot waterfall beneath her feet. Mists from the churning waters bounced off the rocks and splashed her cheek. She wiped the water off her face and jumped ever so slightly to make sure the bridge would hold her weight.

Something strange was happening inside her small body. The roar of the falls became a deafening vibration that seemed to merge with and possess her. The movement of the water and swirling foam mesmerized her. She lost all sense of where she was and whom she was with. For a moment, she felt as if the waters were running through her. Fear stirred inside of her belly, mixing with equal amounts of awe and excitement. She realized that the gentle waters that gave her life in her drinking glass at the dinner table were the same as the waters raging below that could claim her life if she were to jump over the railing. The fear left and the fascination remained.

She wanted to understand this power – the movement and the incredible awesome force of life itself that coursed through her being. She wanted to become one with the roaring waters, to bounce joyfully over the rocks with total surrender, and then divide into a thousand sparkling droplets of mist in the sunshine. She wanted to merge with the river and understand the secrets of its powerful flow.

"Time to go Ann," her father called, interrupting her reverie. She grabbed her daddy's hand and followed him wide-eyed across the bridge, her eyes never leaving the rushing water below. Life had planted a seed within her that would grow over the course of many years. The River had already claimed her for its own.

— § —

Thirty-three years later my tai chi instructor hollers at me, "Surrender! Flow like water!" He should know, I thought. He's had to surrender and flow like water his entire life. Only in recent years was he able to settle down and share his amazing training with those of us fortunate enough to find him.

"Ok," I thought to myself, "flow like water." I mentally focused on what it would feel like to have water flowing through my body – not the throbbing chaos of the falls from my childhood, but rather a meandering river lazily drifting through me. I allowed my hands to rise of their own accord and gently float down to my sides. I breathed in and out very consciously as my feet moved in rhythm with the rest of my body. In an instant, I was flowing like water, surrendering to the power I had worked so hard my whole life to understand. This power took over my motions, gently swaying my arms and legs as I continued to breathe and empty my mind. The energy running through my body felt like warmth that radiated from my belly. Soft tingles of electricity flowed like water through my arms, hands, legs, and feet. I felt the energy flowing through my heart. My whole being began to buzz in unison with the humming of the night insects, the soft flickering of the lamps on the lawn, and the gentle rhythm of the eucalyptus trees swaying in the breeze. The feeling was very much like being in love.

I have come to understand the energy that runs through our bodies as the force of life itself. This energy is the River of Love, and its movements are the currents of Divine grace. This energy is the breath of God that breathes life and meaning into our being. This energy is the same energy that flows through all of creation – the rocks, plants, animals, oceans, weather patterns, and minds of men and women alike. This energy is what creates health, happiness, inspired ideas, and ideals when allowed to flow freely. The same force causes illness and dysfunction when its flow is restricted.

The River of Divine Love provides the intelligence

that causes a cut to heal, triggers an acorn to grow into an oak, and governs the movements of stars in the heavens. Science studies mechanics. Spirituality seeks motivation. Nonetheless, the River is both "quantum field" and "breath of God." Our labels are irrelevant. What is important is whether you choose to acknowledge the River, surrender to its presence in your life, or ignore it entirely. This determines your very tangible day-to-day experience of life as one of grace and ease or one of intense struggle.

I have wondered about this force my entire life. Ever since my moment at the falls, I've been curious about the powers that move us, run through us, shape us, and seem to direct our lives.

As an adult I've often wondered how some people are given the grace to pick themselves up time and again to create a blissfully happy life after numerous trials, abandonment, betrayals, and disappointments, while others seem to give up, become embittered, and give in to a lifetime of suffering.

Consider these examples:

- A client of mine endured the death of her grown daughter, her husband's infidelity, a divorce, and the death of her mother over the course of a few years. With incredible courage and bravery, she sought help and faced the internal demons of fear, pain, anger, and panic to emerge from the process with great faith, a strong connection to her deceased mother, forgiveness for her ex, and a string of admirers. In fact, she dated several sweet men before marrying an incredible man who adores her. Life continues to challenge her, but she faces every instance with amazing grace. What distinguishes this amazing woman from another client with a successful career and supportive family who remains depressed?

- Why does the single mother of two, who left home when her husband was threatening to kill her, always believe her needs will be met (and they are), while the seemingly happy couple with the house on the hill cheats on

each other and worries about their next
paycheck?

*   Why does a successful entrepreneur sell his
    business to travel and seek out the real
    stirrings of his soul, while another insists on
    working himself to death?

*   How can a woman who was tragically raped in
    childhood, abused by so-called therapists, and
    diagnosed with "Dissociative Identity Disorder,"
    work diligently to emerge from her tragic past,
    whole and healed with an open mind and
    compassionate heart, while another woman
    cannot even forgive a petty disagreement with
    her own sibling?

I've come to believe the answer is simpler than I
would have expected.

*Some souls intuitively know how to recognize and
embrace God's grace while others miss the incredible
opportunities for Love available in each moment.*

Over the last several years of my life I have learned to embrace this truth so deeply that it has transformed my life. Let me repeat it once again:

Grace is available every single moment of your life.

I want to share this wisdom with you so you too can transform your life into a magical exploration of God's Love. I want to help you see how you are never alone, never unloved, and never without guidance.

I want you to know that God loves you so very much, that in every second of every day, in every breath you breathe, in every beat of your heart, Divine Love, wisdom, guidance, and healing flow through your mind, body, spirit, and emotions. Divine Love informs your cells, your mind, and your heart. The River of God's Love and grace motivates your anger and your joy, your sadness and your bliss, your health and disease, your catastrophes and your triumphs.

You are never alone. You were never meant to

handle life's challenges without support. You were never intended to face a long night without the company of angels, nor were you ever expected to take care of everyone else around you. Before you were born, God devised a system of support so strong, so all-encompassing that you would never have to be without Divine Love. The only problem with this system is that it is so obvious that most of us barely notice the subtle currents of the River. We forget how to feel Divine Love, embrace it, cooperate with it, and receive it. We get lost in the illusion that we are separated from God. We have to unlearn a great deal of our conditioning to remember the ease with which we can embrace grace.

As a result, we struggle so often against our own hearts. We have been trained to handle the things we "should" do, while we deny our soul's desires. We should listen to a friend who is complaining about the same situation for the umpteenth time, but we really want to read a book. We should take care of our aging parents who have plenty in retirement but don't want to spend it "just in case," but we really want to spend the money on a new business venture. We should work hard and save money, but we long to take a leave of absence and create works of art. We feel we should worship God in a building with a community of others, but we also long for a more personal and passionate connection with the Divine. We've learned to "be good," "make nice," and sacrifice our own well being for the illusion of helping others.

I have heard all these "shoulds" and a thousand more in my practice as an angel communicator and spiritual coach. I have seen these "shoulds" suck the very life force and passion out of my clients, and I have seen the passion and spirit return when these individuals begin to reconnect with the River of God's Love as it flows through their own hearts. God isn't in your life to take care of what you think you "should" be doing with yourself. God is here to breathe life into the beautiful soul that you are. God is here to help you express Divine qualities in the world whatever they may be, through you. God is working in your life to help you be *yourself* and no one else. As you allow this miracle to occur –

the blossoming of your own unique self-expression – you will help and inspire others more than you would ever have believed possible. After all, God created the miracle that is you.

Some of you were meant to be great spiritual mentors; others are masterful mothers. (Really, is there a difference?) Some of you wished to express your heart through art while others are here to elevate our ideas and engineer new technologies to make our lives easier. Some of you are lovers learning to be strong for yourselves and others are fighters learning to lay down the sword, release the struggle, and surrender to Love. Some of you are shy and quiet and would rather express your Divinity in silent prayer, while others are driven to speak in public. Each of you has a spark of Divine light that is your soul, trying to grow into a brilliant beacon of expression. The River of God's Love is always whispering to you, trying to get your attention to guide you on a path of self-discovery, an ever-expanding understanding of Divine Love in your own heart, and a life of joyous abundance.

So, what are these waters – the currents in the River of Love? They are the subtle energies that move throughout your body that you can learn to feel, as well as the not-so-subtle illnesses, injuries, and pains that cry out for attention. They are the gentle and sweet desires of the heart, and the raging torrents of emotion that occur when you ignore these desires. The currents place soft whispers of guidance in your mind or cause your entire life to fall apart if you are ignoring the answers to your prayers. These waters are the events that steer you into a blissful relationship or the guidance that has you find an immature or abusive partner with whom you will be challenged to grow in self-love. The currents in the River of Love are varied and many, and each one has a unique way of guiding you in your life.

Divine Love is the current always present in the depths of the River. Love flows through the deepest parts of your own heart and soul. You will always find Love beneath the stormy or calm surface of your life, without exception.

In this book, we'll explore the many ways that Love informs and guides you. You'll learn how to sense and feel subtle energies in the body. You'll begin to recognize and resolve issues that cause pain before you have to experience illness. You'll discover the value in all emotions and learn how to decode their messages from your soul. You'll learn to surrender to both the chaos and the stillness in life with peace of mind and heart. You'll learn the value of doing nothing and the joy of being. You'll learn to enjoy the view rather than frantically paddling to get ahead. You'll be taught to dance with divine timing and understand when it is fruitful to ponder a decision versus when your soul wants to take a leap of faith. You'll learn to balance the sacred and the secular and you'll realize that every pursuit is sacred in God's mind.

You'll learn that these waters are nothing less than Love. In addition, when you learn how to flow in the River of Love, you'll understand how to embrace grace. Your life will take on a rhythm of its own that feels natural, unhurried, and productive. Your relationship with *yourself* will become honest and so will your relationships with others.

I may challenge your beliefs about good and bad, right and wrong, and the nature of Divine Love. I may ask you to understand that sometimes the River is peaceful and sometimes rocky, but in all cases, it is Love. I may ask you to ponder why you have chosen struggles in your life and whether or not you are ready to release them. I am asking you to grow, not just to read this book but to absorb its rhythm, do the exercises and allow yourself to flow with your own heart. You may want to read this all at once, or you may quit for a month and come back to it. Honor the River as it expresses through your own heart.

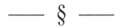

Would you like to put the book down and
take a breather now or do you want to
keep reading? Do it.

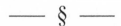

Congratulations! You just passed lesson number one.

Since I left you, a week has passed in my own life. How much time has passed in your own? Did you put the book down or did you keep reading? I congratulate you for honoring your own rhythm. You see, there is a rhythm to everything in life. You breathe in and then out, in and out, in and out, thousands of times a day. The tide creeps up on the shoreline and then recedes. Your hormones fluctuate. Your blood pumps to the beat of your heart. The moon circles the earth. The earth circles the sun, and the sun circles throughout the galaxy in a seemingly endless cycle. All of life occurs in rhythms. The currents of grace in the River of Love are constantly fluctuating. What feels right for you in this moment may change in the next. What is good for your body today may be unnecessary tomorrow. The emotional storm you had yesterday may already have given way to greater peace and understanding.

These fluctuating energies, moods, cravings, and

desires *are* the currents of grace as they flow throughout your body, mind, and emotions. Let us explore these mysterious waters. You will discover that God is very, very close.

II.   Sensing the Currents

The currents of God's Love flow through your physical body, emotions, mind, and indeed your entire life.   You can learn to sense them by becoming very conscious and present to the feelings inside yourself as well as the circumstances around you.

Many of us go about our days according to a rhythm and a schedule that have become routine. We wake up at a certain time, wash our face, brush our teeth, eat breakfast, perhaps go to work, or attend to the family, eat dinner, brush our teeth and go to bed.   We take time on certain days, if we're lucky, for recreation, and we punctuate our existence with special events and meetings with those we love.

When was the last time you were conscious of the first breath you took upon awakening, or the taste of your toothpaste? Do you notice the scent of your morning coffee or the texture of the food you ate for dinner last night? When was the last time you looked into the eyes of your lover, your boss, or even your best friend and wondered what they were feeling in this moment? Are you in touch with your own body, mind, and emotions throughout the day?

Becoming conscious means learning to be attuned to the circumstances and people around you, as well as to the physical and emotional sensations within yourself and the thoughts that course through your mind. Waking up and becoming conscious means you are beginning to take note of where you are, whom you are with, how you feel, and what you are thinking. Eckhart Tolle in his monumental work, *The Power of Now*, says, "Realize deeply that the present moment is all you ever have. Make now the primary focus of your life."[2]

I highly recommend reading Mr. Tolle's book. In order to sense the currents of God's grace in your life, you have to know where you are in the River. If

---

[2] Tolle, Echkart. *The Power of Now*. Novato, CA: New World Library, 1999.

you are stuck in the past – either by regretting what you've experienced or trying to "re-live," rather than "relieve" the events of your past – or if you are overly concerned about the future, you are missing the moment. The subtle currents of grace can only be felt when you are present to your life and yourself in each moment.

I'll never forget the first time I felt the River flowing through my body as an adult. Up until that day, I lived in a very solid and stable reality. Having totally forgotten my experience at the waterfall, I knew myself to be flesh and bone, mind and emotion. I was religious and believed in God, but my upbringing and my engineering background led me to question anything else that I could not see.

That changed the day I met an unassuming woman who professed to be an energetic healer – someone who could manipulate the flow of the invisible electromagnetic fields that emanate from and course through the human body. Not really knowing what to expect, I asked her to show me how she worked. She smiled and simply placed a hand on my shoulder. Nothing could have prepared me for the reality of the sensation I felt next. Heat, electricity, and a tingling sensation shot from her hand, into my shoulder, all the way down my left side, through my foot and into the floor. I stared at her as if stupefied, and she proceeded to show me how her hands emanated a soothing heat that seemed to relax any spot they touched. I had been struck by the proverbial lightning of insight – not simply by her energy but rather by the realization that I was indeed much more than the solid creature I witnessed in the mirror every day.

I proceeded to work with healers, shamans, and mystics to learn more about this invisible life force that runs through all of us. I now feel the subtle energies so strongly around others and in my own body that if I were to disconnect from this sensation it would be as devastating as losing my sight or hearing. I have learned to tune into a deeper way of sensing life, and so can you.

Recognizing the flow of invisible energies in your

body is simply learning to sense something that has always been there. Consider this analogy: When you listen to a song on the radio, chances are likely that you instinctively notice some aspects of the song more than others. For example, you may be a person who remembers lyrics. Others will have an easier time focusing on the melody. A drummer would intuitively notice the percussion.

If you were to study music however, you would find that each song is a rich tapestry of many components that are artfully woven together. See if you can listen at a deeper level next time you listen to a song. Notice the lyrics for a moment, then change your focus, and tune into the melody. See if you can pick out the instruments playing in the background. Can you deepen your awareness and notice the timing of the song – the changes, the rhythm, the pauses, etc.? Note the volume level of the singer(s) as compared to the volume of the music. As you learn to focus more deeply on any given song, you will experience its richness and gain a deeper appreciation of its complexity. Try this exercise with a song you have heard many times, and see if you can deepen your experience of listening to music by being more conscious.

Likewise, as you learn to consciously pay more attention to the physical sensations in your body and the instinctual feelings that have always been present, you will become more attuned to the presence of the River as it runs through your own body and the bodies of others.

The reality of this energy is no longer a secret guarded by mystical traditions that lie behind the major world religions, nor is it simply a "woo-woo" belief of the new age community. Both science and mystics now agree that there are electromagnetic fields generated by and surrounding the physical body. When you were first formed in your mother's womb, an electromagnetic field developed around your spinal cord that helped give direction and guidance to the growth of your organs and the rest of your tiny body.[3] Athletes use devices that generate subtle currents to help bones heal faster. The electromagnetic fields emanated by the body

---

[3] Gerber, Richard. *Vibrational Medicine.* Rochester, VT: Bear & Company, 2001.

can be used to diagnose disease. In time, energy medicine will continue to expand and elaborate upon what the mystics have always known – energy in balance and in motion is healthy energy. Stagnant or sluggish energy tends to indicate disease.

If the River, "chi," "life force," "breath of God," or "spiritual energies" are flowing through your body in an unobstructed manner, you will experience incredible health and vitality. If the flow is obstructed in certain areas, you will more easily attract accident, injury, or disease in those areas. While illnesses are most certainly biological in nature, in most cases there are fairly predictable emotional patterns that make a person susceptible to them. Allowing yourself to feel your emotions does not cause disease, but repressing or ignoring them can.

Again, this is not such a mystical concept after all. Suppose your parents yelled at you every time you tried to express yourself as a child. Throughout your life whenever someone looks displeased, chances are likely you will hunch your shoulders and clench your jaw to keep from expressing what you really want to say. You'll learn to "make nice" with everyone, secretly building up a lot of resentment and pressure because no one important to you seems to notice or even care about what you want to say. The anger in the jaw becomes pronounced; you develop TMJ or a stiff neck. You may get migraines, and you wonder what on earth is wrong. This is a case of your spiritual energies being jammed up, causing your emotional energies to develop into patterns that don't feel authentic, which in turn creates physical discomfort or dis-ease.

When I hold my hands above someone else's palms, I feel spiritual energies moving through them that tell me if they are joyful or angry, sad, lethargic, or scattered. When I move my hands above an individual's body, I sense areas where the River is not flowing so well, and these often prove to be areas of discomfort or disease. When I quiet my mind and focus on different areas in my own body, I can sense the currents and discover how they are related to the thoughts and feelings in my own mind and heart.

This ability to sense the River is not a sixth sense accessible only to a few gifted souls, but rather an extension of the five senses that you already have. With practice, anyone can learn to sense the subtle energies.

As you learn to pay more attention to what is going on in and around you, you will become attuned to the River's subtle currents. The easiest place to begin sensing the currents of the River is within your own physical body. Take a moment and try this exercise:

—— § ——

Sensing Energy – Part 1

Becoming Aware

Sit or lay comfortably where you will not be interrupted for a few minutes. Focus on your breathing. Don't change it or try to breathe more deeply. Pay attention and notice how deeply your breath travels into your lungs. Does it go deeper into one lung than the other? Are your sinuses open or blocked? Do you breathe through your mouth or nose? How does your body feel when you inhale? Note how you feel when you exhale.

Next, slow your breathing down and allow it to become very conscious and very deep. Adjust your posture to see if you can breathe more deeply and evenly into both lungs. Don't force the air into your lungs. Allow it to travel deeper by relaxing.

See if you can keep relaxing your back, throat, and neck to allow more air in and out. Do not push the River. Release control. Relax deeper. Perhaps you need to adjust your neck, drop your shoulders, and release the tension in your hands. Perhaps you need to shift your weight, lean to one side, or lay on your back. Experiment until your breathing feels deeper.

Notice how you feel now as you inhale very slowly. Pay attention to your body as you exhale as well. Was there a difference between your normal patterns of breath and how you felt when you chose to breathe more consciously? Make a note in your journal about what you experienced.

— § —

Chances are likely that you felt differently when you began to pay attention to breathing deeply. Many people report that their first deep breaths require effort. Their muscles are not yet accustomed to breathing deeply. They are trying to force air into their lungs. As you learn to relax, however, and practice deep, slow breathing, something magical happens. You begin to allow the River to breathe for you. If you continue this exercise just a few minutes each day, there will come a time when you stop trying to breathe deeply and your breathing develops a natural and deeper rhythm of its own. You are feeling God's breath. You are surrendering to a higher power.

Try the following exercise to deepen your surrender:

— § —

Sensing Energy – Part 2

Surrendering to the River

Sit comfortably once again and simply notice your breath. If you have done the previous exercise a few times, it should be deeper and slower now. Do not attempt to alter your breathing in any way except to adjust your posture to become more comfortable. Let go of control. Simply notice the gentle rush of air into your lungs and the gentle release. Simply become aware.

Do this for several minutes. Feel the pleasure in your body as the air travels deep into your lungs. Use your imagination to perceive the oxygen enriching your bloodstream and nourishing every single cell. With each inhale, allow the oxygen to travel throughout your body, enlivening you. With each exhale, relax into the sensation of releasing control. Simply observe. You are not making any of this happen.

— § —

If you did this exercise without trying to control your breathing you will notice that at some point you feel as if you are not the one doing the breathing but rather as if a force larger than you is breathing for you. God, in an ongoing creation of His love, breathes through you. The more you let go of control over your breathing, the deeper you will breathe. The more you surrender to God's Love, the deeper you will feel it. The more you choose to cooperate with the urgings of your heart, the more you will operate in harmony with creation, release struggle, and feel the joy of being in the flow.

God's breath is the breath that we breathe. The easiest way to begin sensing the energies that make up the currents of the River is to surrender and relax into your natural rhythms as you practice breathing more slowly and deeply. As you inhale, you breathe in a little bit of all that is. As you exhale, you contribute a little bit of your own unique energy back to the world. The oxygen in the air you breathe may have been in the ocean's waters, evaporated into clouds, and rained down up on the earth, absorbed by the roots of a tree in the rainforest, exhaled by the tree back into earth's atmosphere, blown by the currents of the earth's motion and weather patterns to your neighborhood, and finally taken into your lungs. The waters in the ocean were formed during the creation of earth itself, whose raw matter is believed to have come from the stars. So where does the breath truly begin and end? Our breathing is one of the most obvious and yet overlooked connections to eternity. God didn't really intend to hide His presence. The River of Love, of life itself, flows through you with every breath.

— § —

Sensing Energy – Part 3

Discovering flows and blockages

Breathe again. Allow yourself to feel the River of God's Love and eternal nature coursing into your lungs and throughout your entire body. Allow your breathing to be easy, natural, and relaxed. Once again, adjust your posture until you feel more open and comfortable. As you allow your breathing to occur and simply observe it flowing in and out, use your imagination to assign a color to this flow of air. Shut your eyes and imagine what color the energy flowing in and out of your body might be. Imagine this energy flowing throughout your body with each breath. Use your inner vision and imagination to scan your body slowly and deliberately and notice where this flow seems to be blocked. Don't try to change this for now. Simply notice.

— § —

Questions for Reflection

1. As you breathed, did you notice heat in any areas of your body or were there spots that seemed tight and cold?

2. Did you experience any subtle and pleasant tingling or electrical sensations anywhere in your body?

3. Did you find yourself feeling as if the energy wanted to adjust your posture or were there spontaneous movements or adjustments that

occurred as you were breathing?

4. What color was the energy that runs through your system? Don't worry about assigning meanings to the colors. They simply make it easier for you to visualize the River's energetic currents. In time, you will define what the colors represent to you.

5. Did you perceive any blockages to the flow? If so, where were they and what do you perceive them to look like?

Congratulations! You are learning to sense the River! The heat, tingling, strange but noticeable feelings of movement, and other interesting sensations are the subtle currents of energy flowing through your body. The tight and uncomfortably cold spots are often areas where the energy is not flowing so smoothly.

If you like, you can also learn to see the subtle energies of the River. One of my first experiences with spirit guides occurred when I shut my eyes and was given a vision of my world as energy rather than solid form. I saw rivers of light pouring through all of creation, forming the shapes we know of as rocks, plants, and trees. As quickly as the vision came, it left, but I never forgot the beauty of the River of God's Love that gives everything life.

When I practice seeing energy, I can find that focus and the colors pop into view; however, this is not something I have been disciplined with. I see energies only intermittently at present. As I practice more, I see more.

Here are a few exercises to help you see:

— § —

Seeing Energy – Part 1

The Subtle Glow

This exercise is rather well known because it works. Sit still and do the breathing exercises as before until you become very calm and focused. Wait until you are relaxed enough to feel the energy moving through your body. Now, rub the palms of your hands together very briskly and then move them together and apart, not quite touching. Play with this until you begin to feel the sensation of energy between them. You might perceive this as heat, tingling, or a slight sticky sensation. When you reach this point, turn both palms towards you. Line up the fingertips of both hands to point at one another. Move your fingers together and apart, loosely focusing at the space between them. Don't look straight at the space in between but rather let your gaze be very lazy, as if you are staring beyond the space. This exercise is easier to do if you are moving your hands in front of a very light or very dark solid background.

If you keep this up, you will eventually see colors, lights, or maybe a little wispy looking smoke-like substance between the fingertips. You are seeing energy.

— § —

Seeing Energy – Part 2

Watch your lights shine

Move a comfortable chair in front of a
large mirror such as a bathroom mirror
or a dressing room mirror. Sit
comfortably and breathe as before.
Sense the energy moving throughout
your body. Loosely focus at a spot a few
inches above your head. Let your gaze
relax and look as if you are staring far
away through this spot. Keep the focus
loose. Breathe. Relax. Release any self-
judgments. If you keep trying patiently,
you will eventually see a clear haze or
even colors above your head and around
your body. You are seeing your own
aura! At first, you may only see clear
light or certain colors, but if you keep

practicing, other colors will eventually come into view.

God's Love flows through your body in the form of subtle currents of electromagnetic energy that pulse with the natural flow of your breathing. Just as blood runs through your physical veins, the energy runs throughout your body as a River of light. Your soul's energy tends to enter and leave through the solar plexus, a spot a few inches above your navel. This is the same energy center where people vie for power, "yank your chain," and "push your buttons." This is why we often cross our arms over our stomach when we feel defensive and protective, and why we have "gut" instinct. We process most of our emotions in this area of our body.

It is not a wonder that sensitive people often have issues with digestion. People with bulimia have often swallowed too much negativity from one parent and not received enough emotional nourishment from another. They use food as a substitute for nourishment, and then their body rejects the excess they have swallowed. People with disease of the colon have a hard time letting go of others' "you know what." When we get nervous, we pull the energy into our solar plexus very quickly and often feel queasy. When we fall in love, the energy rushes into us effervescently, giving us the sensation of butterflies. This energy is very real and affects us on a day-to-day basis. Caroline Myss, a wonderful spiritual teacher and mystic, has a set of tapes entitled "Energy Anatomy"[4] that describe the flows of energy in the human body and its primary energy centers in great detail. This is a fantastic course of further study if you are interested in learning more on this topic.

Ideally, the River flows through you in an unobstructed fashion, bringing God's Love and life force to your muscles, bones, organs, and all physical systems. In the ideal world, God's Love washes through and animates every cell of your body completely with every breath. You age more

---

[4] Myss, Caroline. *Energy Anatomy*. Boulder, CO: Sounds True, 1997.

slowly, remain healthy, and for the most part, feel more joyful.

However, life is not always ideal. Most of us have developed both physical and emotional issues that keep the energy from running through us freely. For now, simply notice the areas in your body where your energy seems sluggish or blocked. Be gentle and non-judgmental as you learn to perceive the River's flow through your body. You are waking up to a greater awareness of life. Practice. Learning to notice the River takes time. You'll learn how to eliminate these obstructions in a later chapter.

The process of becoming more conscious and aware is a form of meditation. Meditation is simply doing whatever it takes to become 100% present. You can become present doing anything that forces you to pay attention to what is happening right now. You are likely to be naturally present to life when you engage in an activity you love, when you're with someone you simply adore, or in a situation that commands your complete attention. You can learn to be present in any life situation.

As you practice sensing energy, you'll find that you also become more aware of your feelings and the details of life around you. You might realize all of a sudden that the cereal you've been eating for breakfast for the last ten years doesn't really thrill you. You might wake up and see for the first time how tired your spouse looks and that he or she needs a little extra love. You might notice a lovely tree that you've passed numerous times on the way to work but have never taken time to see and appreciate. You might see the adoration in your child's eyes or notice how he or she is hungry for your attention.

As you practice becoming more aware, you'll notice more of the still, small voices inside of yourself. You might discover that you can no longer deny the urge to investigate a new career, pursue a new hobby, or quit engaging in an activity that has become routine. You might find that a situation you once put up with is no longer tolerable. You might fall in love all over again with the partner you've inadvertently begun to take for granted.

There are so many ways you can become present to life. Breathing consciously is certainly one of the simplest methods I've found. If you practice the exercises in this chapter consistently, you will trick yourself into learning to meditate. You'll learn to become present to the sensations in your body and to your own subtle thoughts and feelings as well. In addition, you'll become more aware of life around you, and therefore, more aware of the River's guidance.

I'll never forget an incident when the angels showed me some of the simplest benefits of being present to life around me. I was sitting impatiently in my car in traffic, stopped by a red light, and feeling very frustrated by what seemed to be yet another delay in completing my errands for the day. As I waited for what seemed to be an eternity, the angels decided to teach me a lesson. "Ann, you haven't even noticed the rocks in the median," they told me. "What rocks?" I thought. I looked out my window and found to my surprise that the median was indeed paved with beautiful river stones. I had driven past this spot hundreds of times and never noticed. "Be present with the rocks," the angels advised. I went along with the exercise. I stared at the median, silenced my mind, breathed slowly, and just sat there contemplating the beauty of those rocks. All of a sudden, visions of the river where the rocks originated popped into my head, and then I saw the volcano that tossed them out of the earth before they were tumbled by the waters. I fast-forwarded in my mind and saw the laborers who had gathered these rocks, the trucks that had hauled them, the service people who had cataloged and priced them, and the men who had laid them in the concrete median. I felt very connected to life and instantly relaxed. The traffic light turned green and I went about my day in peace.

That exercise taught me a great deal about how we take life for granted when we are not present, and how we miss the Love that is available to us in each moment. I wonder if God knew, millions of years ago when He designed the volcanoes that would carry these rocks from the heart of the earth, that a woman in our time would learn a lesson in gratitude from them, write about them in a book, and perhaps share a little inspiration with others. There is continuity to life's design that is greater than we could ever comprehend. It is important only to be present to our place in the River, and therefore, the currents that guide us. Then, we will know whether to sit still or move, remain silent or speak, what to do, when to do it, and where to go next. Then, we will operate in harmony with all of creation. Then, we will feel God's great love throughout our days.

To sense the gentle currents of the River you simply need to practice until you can become inwardly still enough to notice what is going on inside and around you. The more you practice, the more you will notice subtle energies, thoughts, emotions, whispers in your heart, psychic signals, and so forth. Congratulate yourself. You are waking up to a much greater experience of reality.

III. Gentle Currents & Raging Rapids

Just as an author gives birth to a book, the book gives birth to the author as its truth unfolds in her life.

Today, as I write this, the current of grace in my life is a fractured left foot, a ripped tendon, nerve damage, and a recovery period of about six months. I wasn't listening to the gentle currents of the River via the whispers in my own heart; instead I needed a jolt in my life to wake me up and remind me that God's Love and purpose included me and my own heart's desires, not only those whom I serve.

I study Tai Chi and Kung Fu with a group of amazing people. Some of them are learning how to do what I call "Crouching Tiger/Hidden Dragon" leaps. Standing still, both feet on the ground, they breathe deeply, gather their energy, and launch themselves onto tree stumps that have been sawed off to make a platform 34 inches above the ground. They are jumping a distance over half my height. My instructor was very clear when he told me I wasn't ready to try this move. "You're not strong enough yet," he assessed. The insatiable (and insane) desire to ignore all reasonable human limitations arose within me. This was the same habit that had me helping others during my spare time instead of getting a good night's sleep, and answering phone calls during my lunch break instead of slowing down to eat a leisurely meal. It was this same thinking that caused me to buy gifts that my friends couldn't afford for themselves instead of saving for my own goals. It was the old program that motivated me to run errands during my days off instead of listening to my heart that longed to be outdoors and dream a kinder and gentler life into existence.

"I want to try!" I told a friend of mine, referring to the jump. "Now?" he asked, after class, looking at me a bit incredulously. We trained for an hour and a half and had just sat down to chat. "Sure!" I answered excited as a puppy. I knew my right side was balanced and strong. I leapt and easily landed on my right foot, very excited to have accomplished the jump. I eased myself back down to the ground and considered whether I could achieve the same leap with my left foot.

I wasn't so cocky anymore. I was off balance and I knew it. I was present with myself enough to recognize the little naggings of doubt that were trying to keep me from injury. "I'm not so sure about this," I said hesitating. A split second of grace offered me a gentler course of action. I heard the subtle stirrings of one fork of the River – a quiet peaceful way of being that grace offered me, one last time, in that whisper of my heart. My friend echoed my own inner impatience and tendency to push myself. "Come on Ann, you can do it." "I don't know." I said one more time, considering the choice at hand. "Oh what the heck? Why not?" I told myself. I ignored my inner knowing. I chose to push myself beyond my reasonable limits one more time, and in that moment I chose the fork of the River that would take control of my life for the next six months. Over the waterfall I went. Ouch.

Grace occurs first in the quiet desires of your own heart – the subtle stirrings, nagging knowing, inexplicable interests, and disconcerting discontents. Grace comes as a craving for food at your favorite restaurant when you are destined to meet someone you did not know, or the sigh of exhaustion you ignore when you tell yourself, "Just one more email. Just one more errand, just one more..."

A client of mine shared a beautiful story of gentle grace coming through a food craving one night. She had an older home that she wanted to sell, but didn't have the energy to fix up. She also wanted to find a new home but didn't know if she could afford one. "Anyway, what was the use of looking for a new home before she sold the old?" she told herself. Nonetheless, the women knew that God works in mysterious ways, so she prayed for help.

One night, she became possessed with insatiable cravings for a certain dish that she had only heard of, but never tasted, at a restaurant that she hadn't been to in a long time. The cravings were so strong that, uncharacteristically, she decided to go out by herself and get dinner. Even more out of character, she sat at an available table in the bar of this restaurant and invited another single woman who was without table to sit with her. They struck up a conversation, and the River poured into her life. The single woman she invited to her table was looking for a fixer-upper house in her neighborhood, and in no time was buying the first woman's home!

This presented a new challenge of finding a new home, but once again, my dear client put the problem in God's hands. She had been drawn to a community but felt the homes there were out of her price range, so the following Saturday she called a Realtor in the hopes of finding a closeout (bargain) home in some other new housing community. While on the phone with the Realtor, she went the mailbox to pick up her mail. Lo and behold, there was an envelope containing not one but three identical ads for a home in the community she had already admired. This particular floor plan had just been added by the builder and was within her price range. This dear woman took the hint, looked at the home, and knew it was hers. Grace came flowing into her life in a miraculous way via innocent cravings for a dish at a favorite restaurant. She listened to the River. She listened to her own heart.

Grace had been whispering in my life very gently for some time as well. "Ann, you're exhausted." The thought always hit me before I rationalized answering another 20 emails from my clients in need, instead of going to bed at midnight. After all, I was so blessed in my own life! Shouldn't I spend just ten seconds helping a client solve a problem that could otherwise worry him or her for days? It seemed to be the kind thing to do.

"Ann, maybe you should stay home tonight and rest," I would think to myself before pushing myself to get out and exercise. I did love the tai chi immensely; however, I put myself on a rigid schedule that left no room for fatigue or nights off.

"Ann, you never wake up excited these days," I

thought one morning. I had too many activities on my plate to consider why not. The joy had slowly drained from my own life as I helped others find their bliss. I had no weekends dedicated to sitting in silence any time in the near future. In between work and exercise, I was planning a camping trip, looking forward to a house warming party, a birthday party, a graduation party, and numerous other activities. I was not listening to the subtle currents of the River.

I could hear the roar of the rapids approaching, but I ignored what I knew. My friends started advising me to slow down and rest more. My mentors (including the angels I converse with on a daily basis) told me to let my clients solve their own problems except in scheduled sessions with them. My mind was saying, "Yes, yes, I know that's right," but I couldn't resist the drive to assist.

My body started to cooperate with grace's desperate attempt to get my attention. I started having chest pains. I had to go to the chiropractor more frequently for back adjustments, and I had a lot of tightness throughout my body. By this time, I didn't realize I was in the rapids, approaching the roar of the falls.

The gentle sweet side of grace intervened with one last attempt to get my attention, with one nagging feeling that I should not attempt to leap onto my left foot. I was faced with a choice. Be kinder to myself and be free of pain, or slip into old habits and cause more. Stay grounded and balanced or leap into a lesson. Take a gentle fork in the River that was slower and kinder, or rush headlong over the falls. I slipped back into my old patterns, took a bad leap, and did serious damage to my foot.

Pushing the River never leads to a good end. As I write this, grace is now having her way with my life.

I would venture a guess that many of you have shared similar experiences. Most of us at some time or another in our lives have known something deep and true, yet ignored our own wisdom. See if you have experienced one or more of these scenarios:

- Your first impression of a person was a simple knowing that, "this one's not right for me," but out of hope, loneliness, or desperation you talked yourself into giving him or her a chance and ended up in a relationship that wasn't truly right for you.

- You felt excited about an investment or buying a home but got paralyzed with fear or mental chatter and missed an opportunity; or worse yet, you felt uneasy about an investment that someone else convinced you was "too good to pass up" and ended up losing money.

- You had a great idea, but you didn't do anything with it and saw it on the market a few years later with someone else reaping the rewards.

- You secretly know you have a talent, skill, or heart's desire you want to explore, but you aren't willing to do anything about it. The years pass and you don't get any closer to your dream.

- You were feeling claustrophobic or unappreciated at your job shortly before you were laid off.

In each of these cases, the River whispered to you, very gently at first. The River of God's Love is always kind at first, but varies in its intensity as grace attempts to capture your attention.

The first subtle currents of God's grace are the sensations in your body that we discussed in the previous chapter and the quiet whispers of your own heart. They are the feelings of excitement or unease, the nagging knowing that tells you something (or someone) feels right (or wrong) for you, the longing for something more or something new, and the quiet discontents that leave you with a desire to change.

Have you ever felt one of these little whispers?

- You meet someone who you immediately feel drawn to know.

- You begin to feel strangely uncomfortable in an old relationship.

- You see a stranger and have an urge to say something to him or her.

- You know that you "should" run errands, call a client, clean house, but you really want to play, rest, take a nap, etc.

- You keep finding yourself interested in a new hobby or thinking about getting an education in a new field.

- Some old activity of yours that used to excite you is getting boring, tiring, or tedious.

- You are drawn to go to a certain place, see a film, read a book, take a class, or contact a specific individual.

- You have a gut feeling (not a dramatic fear, but just a quiet feeling) that you should check out a health issue.

- You feel as if an angel or deceased relative is near but discount what you know.

- You suddenly want to take a different route to or from work.

- You logically feel a situation looks safe and wonderful but your body tenses up and warns you to pay attention.

- You have fears about doing something you want but every time you think about it, your body feels alive and your heart feels excited.

All of these are examples of the subtle currents of the River. Grace first attempts to get your attention through a gentle knowing or nudging in your heart and mind, and through subtle physical sensations. I've heard many clients come to me complaining that God must be cruel. "How could my life fall apart like this?" they ask me. Upon discussing the matter further, we usually find that they had gentle signs and signals far before approaching the rapids or the falls.

— § —

Questions for Reflection

1. Have you ever "gone over the falls?" Think back to a time when something unexpected and difficult happened that changed the course of your life – for example: losing a job, getting divorced or separated, experiencing betrayal, or having an illness or injury?

2. Did you have "warning signs" before this time? These could include a sense of discontent, physical sensations that were out of the ordinary, being stressed, worrying or being unhappy in a relationship or job, not feeling well, etc.

3. Did you think about doing something to make changes before the challenge? What stopped you – lack of confidence, courage, or expertise or perhaps a fear of the unknown?

4. How did the challenge transform you or your life for the better?

5. What did you learn?

— § —

Luckily, there are many times when we do listen to our instincts, follow up on the desires of our heart (even if only with a heartfelt prayer), or speak up when we feel guided to do so. These are the times when the magic and miracles seem to occur in our lives.

On a recent holiday I was frustrated because I had no idea how I could get myself downtown and brave the crowds with my broken foot. Typically, I attend the city's annual festivities and fireworks celebration with my friends. We park a few blocks away, walk to the area where the celebration takes place, and sit among thousands of people. This year I felt fated to stay at home. Walking a mile from the parking area to the event on crutches in the dark of night was out of the question. I surrendered to my physical limitations and took a nap in the evening instead.

Half an hour before the fireworks were scheduled to begin, I woke up with the brilliant idea that I could get in my car and drive to an overlook high above the city to watch the fireworks from my car.

As I passed a car with a license plate that said NT OOPS ("Not oops" – not a mistake!), I missed my turnoff and found myself headed straight into the crowded city celebration. Parking seemed non-existent, and I resigned myself to the fact that I had to turn my car around and head back. As I turned homeward, I found myself pointed straight into a parking lot I'd missed, complete with open parking spaces. I drove in and asked the attendant how far I would have to walk to see the show. "You can sit in your car lady," he replied, "and look straight up."

What a fantastic surprise! The parking lot bordered the park where the fireworks were set off, and I ended up sitting on a blanket, 10 feet from my car, able to watch the brilliant lights explode in the night sky directly overhead. This was closer than I'd been in all my years of fighting traffic and milling among the masses. I didn't strain my foot. I satisfied my spirit, and I went home feeling the laughter and smiles of the angels who helped me find my way. This is a small but perfect example of listening to the gentle currents of the River simply by paying attention to a simple heart's desire.

Grace is always whispering via the subtlest stirrings of your heart. Consider these other true examples:

- A good friend of mine who never went out to the nightclubs had an urge to go out with friends one night. She became bored and went to stand outside the club. It was there she met the man she would fall in love with and marry years later.

- At one of my summer pool parties, another friend surrendered to her heart and told a new male friend that she liked him. They discovered each other to be a perfect match, enjoyed a sweet courtship, got married, and as of this writing have two beautiful baby girls.

- A client who followed her bliss to play with making jewelry turned her passion into a business.

- A friend listened to her deep heartfelt compassion and helped a stranger who has now become her best friend, business partner, and roommate.

- A woman had a sudden sense of urgency to stay alert on the road and as a result avoided being hit by a truck that swerved into her lane.

- A friend attending one of my seminars decided to follow her heart during an exercise on making requests. One dollar at a time she acquired a sizable donation for a local animal shelter!

The list of major life changes that result from the smallest of choices is endless. We often try to find glorious strategies for making our lives happier, but in truth, the simple and seemingly insignificant choices we make are the ones that most strongly affect the entire quality of our existence.

—— § ——

Questions for Reflection

1. Do you love your job? If not, why are you still suffering through it?

2. Most of you who answered "no" will say you are working to pay your bills. Wonderful! Give thanks that you are taking financial responsibility in your life. Give thanks for the ability to pay your bills, and then in the very next moment choose to honor your heart, jump in the River, and say a little prayer:

    Dear God, I'm ready for meaningful work and a wonderful job. Guide me to a job/career that I can be passionate about, with positive and inspiring people, in a location I love, with hours that work for my loved ones and me, and an income that meets or exceeds my needs.

If this prayer doesn't express your needs, make up one that does. Flow with the grace moving through your own heart. Write your prayer in your journal and put the date right beneath it. You have just begun to create change. You just jumped into the River. Wait for further information or inspiration before taking action. Don't falter in your desire for change.

— § —

Where you end up several years from now depends on the quality and integrity of the decisions you make now, and now, and now, each moment of every single day. You can choose to align your actions and words with your heart, or to stubbornly ignore them. When you align with the heart and inner wisdom, you align with the River. You align with grace. When you ignore the very same, grace will eventually create incredible circumstances in your life to capture your attention.

Aligning with your heart does not always mean making grandiose decisions. The simplest choices are the most powerful. Did you eat lunch when you were hungry? If you did, chances are likely you felt reasonably good afterwards. If not, you may be grumpy or find that your interactions with people are hurried and unpleasant and you can't think straight all afternoon. We operate best when our basic needs are met

Did you get enough sleep last night? If not, what can you do to change that? Make choices to live a healthier lifestyle because you will feel better. Start simply and slowly with your most basic needs. Instead of telling yourself you'll get to bed an hour earlier, try ten minutes earlier. When you are accustomed to that change, try ten minutes more. Simple choices and simple changes are the most powerful and easiest to accomplish.

Perhaps you have a huge "to-do" list and feel overwhelmed. Your heart may be in need of a little comfort or recreation. Honor that, even if it means taking a 20-minute nap, reading ten pages of a book, or going outdoors for a little sunshine and fresh air. You will find your energy replenished and your desire to accomplish the things you must do rekindled.

The heart and inner wisdom cannot be ignored if you want grace in your life. Grace is to the spirit what water is to the body. You cannot live happily without either one.

— § —

Questions for Reflection

1. Write down a time in your life when you did listen to your heart or your gut instinct.

2. Did you know the outcome, or did you simply feel compelled to act, speak, or try something new?

3. What motivated you?

4. How did the situation turn out?

5. Were you happily surprised or did things seem to go wrong in spite of honoring your own instincts?

— § —

At this point you may be wondering what went wrong at certain points in your life when you did follow your heart and things didn't turn out as expected.   What about the relationship that promised a bright future but turned out to be your biggest challenge?   What happened when you started the business you loved only to see it fail?   How is it you felt surely guided to make a move and found yourself without friends?

What I've witnessed time and again in my work with clients and in my own life is that dreams gone awry usually start with the person following his or her heart, but get misdirected as the mind begins to usurp the heart's power. You jump in the River but instead of floating on the meandering currents, you try to maintain your original course. Grace is not static. Rivers don't flow in straight lines.

Consider the last time you fell in love. You were honoring your heart in the moment you decided to go out with the person you admired. Grace was either guiding you to get into the relationship of your dreams, or perhaps a lesson in how you sell yourself short, give yourself up, fall in love for the wrong reasons, or allow yourself to be abused. You did the right thing. You jumped into the River.

With each moment you spent together however, the relationship either got better or worse. You either communicated from your heart or stuffed your feelings. You either chose to behave in a loving way, or you were buried in insecurities from your past and worries about your future. With each choice, the relationship grew closer together or farther apart. I am not saying you are solely responsible for the character of your relationships – as the old saying goes, "It takes two to tango." However, it only takes one to choose love. Moreover, the one choosing love and deep levels of honesty will end up in a loving space whether or not the relationship lasts. If you kept listening to the currents of grace after you took your first leap, you would have grown gracefully and known whether or not the relationship was to be continued or released gracefully with lessons learned.

In the case of relationships gone awry, there was a time you knew things weren't working as you had hoped. At that moment, did you choose to express the truth in your heart, based on the reality of the other? Did you consider getting help or leaving? Or more likely, did you fall into wishful thinking that things would change, try to manipulate or coerce the other into doing what you've wanted, or worse yet, start making yourself wrong? No judgment here – I've done all three! Most of us, at some point in our lives, have tried to change ourselves or "fix" someone else. We've tried to make others understand us. We've urged, cajoled, manipulated, sweet-talked, bullied, or bribed, instead of simply saying, "I love you, but this behavior doesn't work for me. Is there any possibility of compromise?" If there is, wonderful! If not, you have discovered differences and can make more informed choices together. The River always encourages impeccable honesty. Anything less will make you feel as if you are drowning in a sea of confusion and chaos.

The gentle currents of grace can be found in your heart and in your body, but only when you are willing to deal with the reality of life, yourself, and others. Wishful thinking, insecurity, jealousy, fear, denial, and judgment all disconnect you from your heart and the sensations in your body. Before you decide to speak or take action, get help getting out of drama and get in touch with the reality of life around you. A job, a relationship, or a behavior either works for you or it does not. Either change is possible or it is not. Either others are willing to cooperate or they are not. Wishing life were different or focusing on the unrealized potential in a situation or person wastes precious time and energy and sends us whirling into the confusion of our minds, instead of resting peacefully in the clarity of our hearts.

Many of our poor choices result from taking action or speaking when we are not connected with our hearts. Most of our good choices result from taking action or speaking based on the clarity of heart, married with the logic of the mind.

In other words, you have to be impeccably honest about where you are in the River before you can decide the best way to navigate its currents.

— § —

Questions for Reflection

1.   Are there any areas of your life where you are in denial or lying to yourself or others on a regular basis? For example, are you pretending something is ok, when in reality it is not?

2.   If so, admit to yourself and God right now what you really want out of the situation. God does not judge our desires – it is Divine Love that places them in our hearts for us to discover.

     For example, if you are in an unhappy relationship, be honest – you want a good one! You are not telling God to change the person you are with or to make him or her go away.

You are simply taking the first step here in admitting you desire change. What you do next depends on the situation – seek counseling, speak from the heart, or become more compassionate. If you honor the heart in each moment, you will find the way to transform your life.

IV. Sinking, Swimming, & Sailing

If you wish to stay afloat in the River, you must be present to the circumstances of your life. A rafter cannot navigate the rapids while wishing to be in gentler waters. There must be focus on the moment at hand. Denying your present situation or your feelings about life is a useless waste of energy and the quickest way to drown in the River.

What do I mean by drown? Simply this: If you are in denial or not in touch with the truth of your heart, life will present situation after situation, circumstance after circumstance, or relationship after relationship to force your truth back up to the surface. Only when you are in touch with your own heart can you navigate the River with grace and ease.

A client shared this with me: She had been in three

marriages with men who refused to take their share of responsibility. Her heart longed for someone who would love and cherish her, but she buried her feelings and tried to tell herself that things would get better. However, the River always dredges up truth. In time, she realized she could no longer convince herself that these immature relationships were acceptable. After her third divorce, she got real with herself. "I saw all my friends married to rich doctors who adored them," she told me, speaking of her moment of truth with a wonderful candid sense of humor. "I finally said, 'God, that's what I want. Why not me?'" I grinned as the angels whispered the outcome of her story to me. She smiled too. "Yes," she said, "My new husband is a successful doctor, and he's wonderful!"

The River will guide you time and time again into situations that force you to be impeccably honest with yourself. Divine Love wants you to be happy, fulfilled, expressed, loved, and secure, but sometimes you're guided to experience just the opposite until at long last you truly own your desire for better. You fight the River when you lie to yourself. You resist its currents when you feel unworthy of love or support, or guilty for asking too much. If you are guided into enough pain, you will finally insist that you are worthy of joy. Of course, we could all come to these conclusions in an easier fashion, but the human mind is a stubborn creation. We have to deprogram ourselves from the illusions of unworthiness. You may *think* you are worthy, but do you *feel* it? When you truly and deeply own your desires, the River will guide you straight to them and you'll become a great source of inspiration to others.

To "own" your heart's desires, you cannot simply pay lip service to what you want. You have to allow yourself to feel the desire in every fiber of your being. It has to be real. A woman in one of my classes insisted she wanted a job but for some reason, I just couldn't believe her. After a long discussion, she realized that she felt she "should" get a job, when in reality she was enjoying her life as a stay-at-home mom (which in my opinion is a full time job!). Had she insisted on continuing her job search, she would likely have been frustrated with no options at all, or jobs that would have annoyed her until she realized she was happy with her life at home.

The trick to manifesting is allowing yourself to imagine having what you want and to feel the excitement that comes with the vision. Be grateful for your present position in the River and allow yourself to feel the longing for more. "An acorn is perfect unto itself," my angels once said, "yet, it longs to become an oak." We constantly expand our awareness of God's Love and our understanding of our own design. In the process of fulfilling earthly dreams, we learn great lessons of faith, surrender, trust, and compassion. We learn to create in cooperation with God.

During one of my two-month seminars on manifesting your dreams, I realized that I was in need of a new vehicle – hardly a "spiritual" pursuit. My twelve-year-old car was threatening to die at any moment, and I didn't have a clue what I was going to purchase next. I realized Higher Power was going to use me as an example of what could be created when you align your mind and heart with the River of God's Love. I stood in front of the class and declared that I was going to manifest a sport utility vehicle at an affordable price, all the while having no logical idea how this would be possible. I embraced my heartfelt desire for a new car. I embraced the fact that all things are possible with God. I declared my intention to have a new vehicle and trusted the currents of grace to guide me.

I didn't even know what car I wanted; however, soon after I declared my intention, Toyota RAV4's seemed to be everywhere. They parked next to me, cut me off in traffic, and gravitated towards me as if I were magnetized. I saw advertisements for them on billboards, and when I turned on the television, there they were, once again, on the ad playing in front of me. I did my homework and researched them to be sure this was the car I wanted, and then clarified my intention to specify that I wanted a RAV4.

One particularly hot day in August when my old car

was making terribly ugly noises, a particular car dealership in town kept popping into my mind. I drove to the dealership on faith, found they were having a fantastic sale, and within three hours purchased a new car at a rate that I could afford. The whole transaction could not have been easier or more pleasant. I finished in time to meet friends for dinner.

While you might ask, "Why would Divine Love care about a material object such as a new car?" I would answer this: far more than a car, I wanted freedom from worry, safe passage around town, security, and the ability to demonstrate how the process of manifestation works. I had a deep, heartfelt desire for a new car. "Create one and get on with life," the angels informed me. When we admit and own what we want, heaven can help us create it without struggle so we are free to focus on the more important things in life.

Had I not acknowledged my desire for a new car and set the universal wheels in motion through my intent, I would have been burdened by keeping my old car alive and paying for its repairs. Eventually, I would have been forced to buy the new car at a time far less convenient, and most certainly at a higher price. I am very happy I chose to listen to my heart.

The River always offers you choices. You can sink, swim, or sail.

Sinking occurs when you ignore your heart entirely or keep too busy to even feel its longings. The River will force you repeatedly into difficult situations until at long last you own your deeper truths. You will be guided into the relationships you settle for until you're no longer willing to settle. You'll be guided into jobs that demand too much until you put your foot down and insist that you want to be compensated fairly. The River will push you into your own depths until you bring your truth up to the surface. God put those longings in your heart to begin with. They are not selfish.

Swimming occurs when you insist on creating your heart's desires all by yourself. You may own your heart's deepest truths – for example, the desire to succeed at your own business – but you forget to allow the River's currents to carry you. You ignore the smaller longings along the way. You think you have to organize inventory, answer emails, and send out promotional packages to keep your business on track, but you really feel like meeting a friend who has invited you to lunch. If you're a swimmer, you'll decline the lunch and make your business succeed the old fashioned way through a lot of effort and struggle. If you allow the River to carry you, you would meet the friend for lunch who just happens to connect you with a large group of people interested in buying your products. God guides you through your heart. If you acknowledge the big longings but ignore the smaller ones, you will swim in the River.

Sailing occurs when you allow the River to carry you on its currents. You acknowledge each longing in your heart, both large and small; you intend and pray for what you want; then, you wait for guidance before jumping into action. Guidance occurs in those little longings for activities that sound fun and interesting, in sudden urges to call an old friend, and in the craving for a good meal at a certain restaurant. Guidance comes through your heart.

When you choose to sail, you take action only when you feel inspired, motivated, or guided, thus eliminating a great deal of struggle and pain. You learn to achieve a perfect balance of mind and heart. This is the easiest way to live your life. This is where the magic and miracles occur.

To navigate the currents of the River, you must make sure that your heart is your own. I am writing this particular paragraph at an outdoor shopping mall, watching little children ignore signs that they can't read anyway that advise them not to play in the water fountain that springs up from spigots in the ground. Shouts of delight and screams of surprise create a symphony of joy as the water splashes up out of the ground. Some little ones approach tentatively. One girl reaches gingerly into the mists while another sits on the spigots waiting for the fountain's rush. Clearly, these children own their own hearts.

When you were born, you knew your own heart. Before your mind was programmed by family or society, you had no problem crying when you were hungry or tired. You didn't hesitate to reach out for what you wanted or to push away what you did not. Babies don't have any self-worth issues. Unfortunately, upbringing, schools, peers, belief systems, etc., may have trained you to ignore your own inner wisdom. To varying degrees, your mind may have taken over your heart if you have been programmed to please others.

When was the last time you reached for something you truly wanted without analyzing whether or not you were worthy of it, what it meant, and if it was ok to have that heart's desire? It seems our minds are filled with a veritable trash-heap of thoughts, judgments, belief structures, and fears that pollute our simple knowing. It is quite a trick to return to innocence. Yet, without this innocence of knowing our own hearts, we will inevitably be guided to sink into the River until we emerge sputtering and loudly proclaiming our truth.

Within each of you, there are many forms of intelligence. The two we are most concerned about at this moment are the intelligence of the thinking mind (as opposed to Divine Mind) and the intelligence of the heart. The heart's job is to bring you guidance directly from God. The thinking mind is supposed to figure out how to satisfy and follow the heart's guidance.

The heart's language is one of emotion. Emotions are simply energy in motion. Almost every emotion serves a purpose and brings a message from your spirit. If you know how to decipher emotional energy, you can better understand your own heart.

If you feel angry, for example, this is a message from your spirit that something or someone in your life is not in alignment with what you want to experience. Anger is meant to help you take responsibility for your own happiness. Harness the intense desire for growth that lies beneath the anger and you will understand the force that causes a seed to burst out of its shell and push through the dirt into the light. Anger is meant to inspire you to move out of a dark situation. Anger is not intended to be aimed at others.

If you are angry, ask yourself, "What do I need to do or say in order to take responsibility for my own happiness?" If someone is abusive or has hurt you, you need to communicate from the heart, move away from the situation, or get help. Remaining angry does not change a thing and simply implodes an energy that is meant to create movement. Aiming your anger at the other serves no purpose as well. When you recognize that your anger is a desire to be treated kindly, this mandates action. Blaming others for your unhappy situations fosters victimization, feelings of helplessness, and in extreme cases, disease.

Sadness shows us where we are having a hard time embracing life as it is. When you're sad, seek out comfort in healthy ways and focus on accepting whatever has occurred in your life to make you feel badly. Sadness occurs when our minds want life to behave a certain way but the River has pushed us in another direction. We have to let go of our expectations or we will feel torn apart. This is why we feel such lackluster energy when we are sad. We are fighting the River.

For example, I am saddened when people are nasty to one another, and especially when someone is nasty to me. I truly long for a peaceful, cooperative world. However, I can't change anyone. I have to help the people who want help, and accept the fact that there are those who don't want to change.

I was deeply saddened by the suicide of a dear friend. I allowed myself to grieve, and yet gradually I had to accept the reality of her decision. It was something I could not change. True acceptance is the only path to true peace.

Envy shows you where you feel helpless to create what you want in life. You think another person has been graced or blessed but you have not. In reality, you simply have to take charge, intend, focus, and pray for what you want, and stop focusing on your lack. Focusing on lack brings more lack. Focusing on abundance brings more abundance. To remedy jealousy, harness its nuggets of truth – you want something in your life – and put your energy toward creating that. Never begrudge another his or her success. One who succeeds paves the way for others to do the same. If you are brave, ask the person you are jealous of, how they got whatever it is you want. They may even help you towards your dreams.

Loneliness is an emotion that shows us we want companionship, which is a natural human desire. If you want life to reach out and embrace you, you need to reach out and embrace life. Be kind to people when you are out running errands, and chat with people who attract your attention as you wait in line at the grocery store. Find groups of people who are interested in things that fascinate you. Join a church or find a spiritual group that resonates with you. Sign up for classes or volunteer. Join Internet discussions on topics you feel strongly about. The angels often say, "If you want the world to see you, be you." No one is likely to find you if you hide out.

If you love someone who doesn't return your love, consider the fact that your heart longs for what you *perceive* the other to be or what you *imagine* he or she *could* become. Rather than targeting someone who can't, or isn't willing to love you, pray and ask God to bring you a match made in heaven. Trust.

Fear is an emotion that shows us our illusions. Fear shows you where your past has taught you to withdraw from or fight life. When you are in fear, seek healing, the solace of friends, the advice of wise counsel, or at least do deep breathing and pray for God and the angels to help remove the fears. Fear is one of the few truly useless emotions and is the way the denser energies manipulate us and keep us from feeling joy. We think fear protects us from further harm, but in truth, fear dulls our natural senses and ability to discern what is healthy and what is not.

Worry is another feeling that serves little purpose. It is born of fear, not faith and trust in God.

Nonetheless, the angels say that beneath every fear is a love of the thing you fear you can't have or the thing you fear will be taken away. Beneath worry is love as well. Find and acknowledge the love, focus on that, and you will have alchemically transformed these relatively ineffective feelings.

Joy tells you something is right for you. Suppose you absolutely love baking, but you can't possibly eat all you produce. Bake anyway and contribute to a local shelter, or share with people who need a little lift. I love to cook and find it to be a creative outlet, so for Christmas I gifted some very busy and very dear friends with a meal a month. I have found an outlet for my soul's joy and they have more time to relax.

It is important to embrace the so-called negative emotions as well as the positive ones, because they too contain messages from the soul. They show us areas where we need to acknowledge our need to love or be loved. A wonderful book that discusses the value in our "negative" emotions is "The Dark

Side of the Light Chasers"[5] by Debbie Ford. It is one of the first books I've read that doesn't pretend that the darker side of our spirit is outside of God's Love. If the River can't get your attention via the more positive longings of your soul, the currents of grace will push you into circumstances where you feel the heavier emotions. Even this is Love.

The logic of the mind is completely different from the logic of the heart. The mind attempts to label, categorize, and file bits of information. When you encounter a new situation, the mind attempts to find the most closely related experience in its database. In that capacity, the mind is limited. The thinking mind tends to project the past onto the future. It is the equivalent of a computer designed to help you fulfill your dreams. The mind was never intended to run your life. In fact...

... the rational mind is designed to serve the heart.

If your mind serves your heart, you will be in perfect alignment with the gentle currents of the

[5] Ford, Debbie. *The Dark Side of the Light Chasers.* New York, NY: Riverhead Trade,

River. If not, you will be choosing the raging rapids time and again so life's outer circumstances can help (or force) you to get back in touch with your heart.

Take a simple example. I am very excited to be writing this book and yet at this moment, my stomach is growling and I am hungry. My heart, which always wants to take care of my well being, is insisting that I eat lunch. My typical human mind is saying, "Oh come on. Just finish this chapter." However, I can tell I will soon loose focus. My mind can argue with my heart and force me to keep writing or I can save this file, take a brief lunch break, and then resume the task. I choose to honor my heart. I'll be back in half an hour, refreshed and ready to share more...

What does your heart want at this very moment in time? Close your eyes, focus on your heart, and breathe slowly and deeply. Ask your heart to tell you what it wants in this very moment. I am not asking you to figure out your entire future, or even

1999.

solve a problem in your life. I'm simply asking you to ask your heart what it wants right now. Close your eyes and open them only when you have an answer. "Heart, what do you want right now?"

Unless the answer is "to keep reading," put the book down for now and go honor your heart. This could be as simple as admitting you want something that you have no clue how to create. Then, say a simple prayer, and ask everyone you know for ideas or assistance. Honor your heart right now.

— § —

Unfortunately, most of us have minds that are either dominant or submissive, depending on circumstances.

Those of us who have a tendency to push ourselves, ignore our hearts, and use sheer willpower to get through our days have so-called rational minds that are dominant, irrational bullies. Dominant minds have a tendency to prevent you from hearing your heart, because they learned that they must be in control. To remedy this, find time to sit in silence or walk in quiet reflection on a regular basis. Dominant minds usually belong to people who have been rewarded solely for their accomplishments or intelligence early in childhood, or to people who have had to fend for themselves and take on tremendous responsibilities from an early age. Women with dominant minds tend to attract men who want to be taken care of. Men with dominant minds tend to attract women who are dependent as well. Dominant-minded people tend to be highly stressed, fast-paced, over-achievers.

If you have this type of mind, chances are very likely you "push the River." Instead of surrendering to life, you want to be in control. You are trying to swim faster than the current. Instead of allowing things to occur according to their natural rhythms, you form artificial deadlines. You have terribly high expectations of yourself and are likely to be as demanding of others. You are not a bad person. You simply learned that your worth is defined by your accomplishments and ability to get things done.

If you have a dominant mind, your challenge is to take time in stillness, get in touch with your heart, stop "pushing the River," and allow life to unfold without knowing all the answers ahead of time. For years, I had a dominant mind. I prayed for help in surrendering control and learning to trust God. I was so stubborn that it took a broken foot and copious amounts of "down time" to answer my prayer.

Submissive minds belong to those of you who allow yourselves to dream but lack the willpower, drive, or initiative to accomplish the things that matter to you. If you have a submissive mind, you are likely to be intelligent, articulate, and warm-hearted but your dreams never seem to come true. Submissive minds usually belong to people whose dreams were dashed, criticized, or not supported at some point in their lives. Men with submissive minds often attract domineering women. Women with submissive minds tend to attract controlling men.

We seek to balance ourselves, either within or via the outer circumstances of our lives. Submissive-minded people are often prone to despair or feelings of helplessness.

If you have a submissive mind, you might feel as if you are drowning in the River. You know what you want but you have a hard time supporting yourself and you probably don't feel supported by life. Instead of navigating the currents of grace gracefully, you feel as if you are a victim of life circumstances. Again, there is nothing wrong with you. You simply haven't been taught *how* to support your own heart.

If you have a submissive mind, your challenge is to motivate yourself, or better yet, ask for help in taking action to satisfy your heart's desires one small step at a time. This might mean hiring a counselor or life coach, or simply enlisting the support of a friend who will not listen to any excuses.

Keep in mind that these two descriptions of the

rational mind are simply metaphors for your understanding. A perfect marriage of mind and heart occurs when you hear your heart, pay attention to your dreams, and take small steps to make them happen. When the mind and heart are balanced, you are navigating the River to perfection.

Most of us have some areas in our lives where mind and heart are balanced, and other areas where they are not. For example, you may know that you love to be healthy and therefore, you decide to eat moderately and participate in activities that energize you. In this case, you are balanced in the area of health. Nevertheless, in other areas, such as abundance, you may have been programmed that "money is the root of all evil," and therefore you negate or judge your own desires for security and comfort.

Each of us has areas in our lives where the currents of grace are allowed to flow easily and areas in which we are quite stuck. We are learning to allow a graceful dance between the mind and heart. In the areas where the thinking mind and heart are not equal partners, the River will guide us to meet people, encounter situations, and create circumstances to help us learn this delicate balance.

For example:

- If you were taught (or life taught you) that people are unreliable, you will likely go through life circumstances that help you learn to rely on your own wisdom and support yourself before you will believe in and attract a reliable partner.

- If you were taught that you must be overly responsible, you will attract people who make incredible demands of you until you choose to take responsibility for your own happiness, instead of taking care of everyone else's needs first.

- If you were taught that your success or security depends on your bank account, you may face financial struggle or attract a nagging partner until you embrace your intrinsic worth and trust that God provides your security. Only then, you will attract all the money (and the respect) you want and need.

- If you believe that God is a punishing being, you will have to learn to be more lenient and forgiving with yourself and others before you learn to truly embrace God's Love in your own life.

The River will always guide you to find what seems to be missing in terms of the love within you.

While this may seem cruel, it is not. The River of God's Love is always guiding you towards love – greater love of self, greater love and compassion for others, greater tolerance and non-judgment of both. If there is an area inside of yourself that you judge, the River will guide you to revisit that part time and again until you learn to love all that you are.

— § —

Questions for Reflection

1. Do you feel in touch with your heart? If not
    how can you create more quiet time in your life
    to contemplate what you really want? For
    example, you can meditate, walk, exercise,
    cook, sit in nature, or perform any other
    activity that you can do alone and in silence.

    Make a commitment to yourself to spend some
    time in silence each week to allow the desires
    in your heart to arise naturally.

2. Do you take action consistent with your heart's
    desires, if only in the smallest ways? If not list
    a few ways you can seek out support from
    friends, professionals, or others. Make a
    commitment to do one small thing each day to
    come closer to your dreams.

V.   Navigating the River: Times to Float & Times to Paddle

As you strive to create a beautiful dance between mind and heart, you'll notice that there are times spent in active pursuit of your goals (paddling), and times spent in stillness (floating). Most of us have been trained to be comfortable with activity but tend to become anxious and uncomfortable when confronted with the still slow currents of the River.

Nonetheless, even nature reflects the need for periods of activity and periods of rest. Plants sprout in spring, grow in summer, bear fruit in autumn, and go dormant during the winter. Fields must lie fallow to rejuvenate their mineral content. There is a natural pause in between your inhale and exhale during which the energy in your body is distributed and sent to revitalize your cells. Hurricanes have an eye, calm comes before a storm, and waves pull back from the shore, pause gently, and then crash upon the sands once again. Nature realizes the value of its pauses. For us to be balanced and healthy, we must do the same.

"Tubing" on the Salt River is a popular form of recreation during the hot Arizona summers. You rent an inner tube, float it in the river, climb onboard, and drift lazily downstream for as many hours as you can bear to sit still and enjoy the beautiful day. Although there are a few areas where the rapids carry you bouncing over the rocks, most segments of the river designated for tubing consist of gently flowing currents. You come to terms with yourself on the river. If you're always in a hurry to get somewhere, the slower currents will drive you crazy, and you'll paddle furiously in the quiet pools. If you are comfortable with relaxation, you can let the currents carry you, trusting you'll eventually float downstream.

The same can be said for our lives.

Some people have a natural ability to rest when

they are tired, eat when they are hungry, call for comfort when they're lonely, or give themselves whatever it is they need to feel healthy and fulfilled. Unfortunately, many of us were not trained to live this way.

Periods of "down time" are absolutely necessary for balance in our hectic lives. Sadly, society trains us to equate self-worth with "productivity." We feel good about ourselves when we help someone, cross items off the endless "to-do" list, finish a project, make money, walk ten times around the block, and so forth. The challenge is to love ourselves equally if we choose to lay on the couch reading a book for several hours, gaze at the stars, enjoy a leisurely soak in the tub, or sit in the shade of an ancient oak tree while watching the clouds go by.

Congratulations if you are already aware of the deep and glorious truth that your worth in the eyes of God is priceless. You do not have to earn God's Love. It is a constant. The River flows through you and all of creation no matter what you do or do not do.

It does not matter what you build, how much you achieve, how many people you have served, healed, taught, or saved, whether you are brilliant and always right, whether your "to-do" list is always done, or whether you fit one of a million other criteria by which we humans judge ourselves – God loves you no matter what. Happiness is not a product of your achievements but rather a by-product of listening to the dictates of God's Love in your heart. The River of God's Love wants to flow through your life in as peaceful a manner as possible but can only do so if you are willing to tune in to its subtle currents and take time to rest in its quiet pools.

In plain terms, this means you must create time in your life to spend in silence and stillness, or life will create this for you.

An exercise given to me by a spiritual teacher several years ago taught me the value of stillness. This beautiful woman made me sit still for four hours at a time. "Simply sit," she told me. No distractions, no noise, no meditating, no sleeping, no eating, no drinking, and no moving except to use the facilities. Just "be." During those tedious hours, I faced all the anxiety and guilt that I had heaped upon myself when I wasn't doing something. Then something miraculous happened – I broke through the illusions of unworthiness into the bliss that accompanies stillness. I lost all sense of time, felt connected with all of life, and felt a peace I hadn't known was possible. I now love my "down time." I crave stillness.

In the process of healing my broken foot, I found a whole new level of appreciation for these exercises. For the first two months after the injury, I honored the angels' advice. Other than work and bare necessities, I disconnected from the outer world. I cancelled all social activities, turned off the television, radio, and phones. I read no books or magazines and discouraged visitors. I spent hours in silence, pondering the gift of my broken foot, the imbalances in my life that led up to it, and the ways in which I resolved to change. As I "put my foot down" with others who wanted to superimpose their desires upon my life, my physical foot healed. As I rearranged my schedule to create greater balance, I gained strength. As I listened again to my own heart with sensitivity and kindness, the so-called "permanent" nerve damage went away. Life was no longer "getting on my nerves." My life, body, and spirit went through intense transformation.

It is spiritually insane and yet completely common to feel guilty for taking time off. According to the Old Testament, even God rested on the seventh day, and yet, amazingly, so many of us expect more from ourselves. I hear the same comments from clients day after day. "I feel guilty taking down time." "I have so much to do." "I can't take time away from my family. They need me." "I won't make enough money if I rest." Yet, if we don't honor the needs of our own spirit, we cannot give to anyone else with authenticity, and our ability to create abundance will be severely limited. We are pouring from an empty cup.

I'll never forget a dear woman who came to me with one burning question for the angels. "How do I make money," she asked. Her once-thriving business was drying up and she was at her wits' end. I could not get the angels to give me an answer for her. They simply would not respond to her question. She became agitated, and I got frustrated; but after years of talking to angels, I remembered that when I didn't get the answer to a question, heaven had something else entirely to say. I told the woman I would not charge her since I couldn't give her the answer she wanted, and I invited her to stay and hear what the angels did have to say. Out of curiosity, or maybe desperation, she agreed to listen.

The angels came through with a force of love so profound it astounded me. They told her that she had more than enough money saved to live comfortably for over six months. They said she had been burning herself out, working non-stop to keep busy to avoid the pain of a divorce that occurred years ago. She had no peace of mind, and her health was less than ideal. They said she was in such desperate need of rest, recuperation, and healing that God was going to withhold success in any outside venture until she sought out the inner peace that her spirit truly craved. With incredible tenderness, they suggested she embrace this growth gracefully rather than create a true financial and health crisis for herself in the near future. If she took the time to heal, they promised her that her business would once again become successful, and she would be just fine.

She looked at me tearfully and admitted that the angels were right. She desperately needed rest and yet had been afraid to slow down since her husband left her. God bless her, she listened to the angels, healed her sweet heart and was able to move into a much happier, healthier, easier, and more abundant phase of life.

During the still times in your life, if only the stolen moments between meetings, the silent lunches, or the fifteen minutes of quiet time before the rest of the family awakens, you begin to take stock of your position in the River. In these silent moments, you reconnect with who you really are and what you want in life. During these interludes, longings arise from the depths of your heart and guide you to discover your soul's truth. You'll heal deeply, release your illusions, and get back into the gentler currents of the River.

You may have to be creative to carve out a little space and time for yourself. One of my clients lived with her elderly mother in a small apartment. She had no privacy and little time to herself. Her mother demanded nonstop attention during every waking hour and would never have understood the value of "floating" on the River. The only quiet time and space my client could create was an escape into the bathroom each night where she lit a few candles and sat in silence after her mother had gone to bed. During these moments, she discovered ideas for a new career and ways in which she could better interact with her mother. Wisdom came to her while she "floated" on the River. I deeply admire her tenacious spirit.

There have been hundreds of instances in my life when the River forced me to take time to surrender to my own heart – times when I could not, for all my clever attempts, figure out how to push the

River and manipulate God into giving me what I thought I wanted. I learned that I had to slow down and cooperate with the currents of the River before anything in my life would work. I had to learn to float rather than to paddle without direction.

Soon after I quit a stable engineering career to become an angel communicator, I was hired by a local bookstore to be their "psychic in the window." I was barely making enough money to pay my bills and decided to sell a nutritional product on the side to help supplement my income. One particularly long weekend, I sat at a health fair, praying for customers. "I need to sell this stuff, God, please," I prayed. "Hello God. You know I need to pay my bills." No customers arrived. In fact, the more I prayed to sell product, the more people avoided my table. "Come on God. Please! How do I sell more of this?" I prayed, becoming more desperate by the minute. "Go home and take a nap," the angels replied. "You are exhausted." I *was* exhausted beyond belief, but I was determined to stay and make some money. My domineering mind was not about to listen to my heart.

"Go home and sleep," the angels insisted. I felt completely misunderstood by God. Out of sheer frustration and emotional exhaustion, I finally decided to quit and go home. The minute I laid down upon my sofa, I fell into a deep sleep, and while I lay sleeping, several people called to order product. I sold more during my nap than I had the entire two days of the health fair. God was teaching me that my heart matters. The River wants us to have all that we seek, but we have to listen to our smallest desires in each moment. My prayer was answered all along. I just had to listen to my heart to cooperate with God's desire for my well-being.

Around the same time of my life, I went on a beautiful hike and prayed aloud high on a cliff side with the blue sky practically touching my outstretched arms. "God show me how to get my finances back on track." "Forgive your ex-boyfriend," came the answer. "Excuse me God but I'm not talking about relationships, I'm talking about money," I replied, suddenly feeling misunderstood once again. "We know. Forgive him," the angels responded. Forget holiness – I became angry. "Forgive that man? He's horrible. He ran away with the money he owed me. Why that...#$&!*" I felt the angels bemused by my tantrum. "She'll get the point," I heard them say with kindness. "What point? What does he have to do with it?" I practically steamed.

The answer floored me. "Your heart is in chaos. You can't think straight, let alone truly focus on creating new classes to teach. You can barely focus on anything, you are so mad at him. He ran off with some of your money, and you are feeling impoverished because of it. You feel you must work harder because of what he did, and while that is true temporarily, the past is the past. Let it go and give your power to be abundant to GOD once again. You are making him responsible for your condition instead of giving the power to be abundant to God right now. Because of his bad behavior *in the past*, you are giving him power right *now* over your *future*. You have made him your God." Whoa. I shrank under the loving weight of their words then expanded back into truth. I was giving him my power. I was feeling incapable of earning more because he ran off with some of my money. If I forgave, I would have to take responsibility again for my future happiness and abundance. My heart wanted this peace. My mind wanted to hold on to unforgiveness and remain angry.

I chose forgiveness, and everything started moving forward again in my life. I called the ex and told him the debt was between him and God from now on; that I was releasing all ties to him; I was no longer giving him power over my right to be abundant; and that he could carry the lack of integrity on his conscience and explain it to God at the end of his life. A week later, I got a check in the mail. My mind cleared up, and I began to teach classes on manifestation that were extremely popular. The River was teaching me that peace and freedom were what my heart truly longed for.

Several years later, I learned another wonderful lesson in surrender. A friend and I were guided to host an angel conference. Archangel Michael, who has since become a dear friend in spirit, was behind the entire event. How many people should we plan for," we asked him. "Get a room for 300," was his response. "We'll help you." I probably should have realized that meant I could wait for inspiration, but instead I took matters into my own hands and began making phone calls. I was truly inspired to make the first few calls. Although I did not find a room that worked for the event, I did learn about some of my favorite resorts and their facilities. However, when none of these fit my budget, I became desperate and called every resort within a twenty-mile radius. I also called churches, centers, and halls to no avail. Rooms were too big or too small, too ugly or too grand, too pricey, or something else was wrong with them. The calls became drudgery. I realized I was pushing the River.

"Michael, I give up. Please find us a room for the event," I told my dear angel friend. I was tired of struggling. Michael smiled. I temporarily quit looking for conference rooms and returned to normal living.

A week passed with no activity on my part and no inspiration from spirit. Five weeks before the day of the big event no one knew about it! We had no room in which to hold 300 people and without a room we couldn't advertise. Without advertising no one would come. I began to wonder if the conference would take place at all. "You still there?" I asked Michael. "God is handling everything," he replied. A few mornings later I awakened with a crystal clear feeling to call back one of the resorts I had already liked, and although it seemed silly, I listened to the urge. "Hi it's Ann again," I told the conference manager. "I'm just checking to see if you have a smaller room available." "In fact we do," the gentleman answered. "A room that fits 300 just opened up." I felt the angels smiling.

All our earthly struggles cannot achieve what God, with a single stroke of grace, can accomplish when we are willing to surrender to our heart of hearts.

When nothing is working in your life, when you have little inspiration or energy and don't know what to do next, give in to the subtle stirrings of your own heart, no matter how small and insignificant they may seem. Rest and go back to basics. Give yourself permission to indulge in simple creature comforts: a good movie, a healthy meal, a much-needed nap, or a call to a dear friend. Stop paddling against the current of your own heart.

When you honor the heart, your inner state of peace will be reflected in positive and often miraculous changes in your outer world. Don't let programming, guilt, shame, fear, and other people's judgments keep you from honoring your heart. It is your life. "Down time" is infinitely productive to the soul whether those around you understand this principle or not.

If you are on a raft on a River, even when you're not paddling, there is still movement.

You are simply surrendering to the currents that carry you. You are resting while God works behind the scenes in your life. When God wants you to take action, you will know. The urge will be strong within you. The guidance will come from many sources until you take note. Until then, relax and live your life. The angels often beg us not to answer our own prayers. They request that we trust God and patiently allow Him to do the work. The River will carry you to your destinations without struggle if you give up a degree of control.

Unfortunately, we have become masters of trying to manipulate life and others. Out of fear, and a mistrust in God's Love for us, we strategize how to make our dreams come true, push ourselves, and ignore our hearts. I've learned that this type of control is highly overrated. Surrender to your heart, and everything will go more smoothly.

Surrender is not quitting, but rather relaxing into the arms of God.

When you surrender, you trust that God has heard your prayers and that when the time is right you will be guided to take action. Until then, trust that perhaps the movement that your heart requires is not directed outwardly in life. You may require healing, nurturing, attention, comfort, nourishment, rest, recuperation, time to ponder, time to daydream, or time to breathe. Spend quality time with friends. Engage in activities you enjoy. Live your life. God will handle the rest. The River is always in motion.

Surrendering to your heart never leads to changing someone else or trying to manipulate an outer circumstance. Your heart wants feelings and qualities in your life. Your personality tries to figure out how this should look and superimposes its ideas upon the heart. Acknowledging the heart's desires engenders feelings of relief. Focusing on the mind's desires often creates anxiety. Consider these examples:

- A client came into my office professing her love for a man who barely even acknowledged her existence. She wanted him to be "the one" so badly that she hurt from the longing. She insisted that he was what her heart truly wanted.

The angels kindly begged to disagree. They assured her that the truth was that her heart wanted to love and be loved in a beautiful and equal partnership. They pointed out that she was not in love with the reality of this man but rather the fantasy she imagined that she could have with him. In truth he was aloof and, at times, rude to her. They insisted that her heart longed for a kinder relationship.

At first, she didn't want to hear the angels' advice. She wanted him and no one else. She renewed her efforts to impress him, sent him cards, baked for him, and told him how wonderful he was. The more she tried to impose her mind's desires on him, the more he pushed her away.

Several months passed before this sweet woman realized that the angels were right. Her heart wanted love, and this man was not willing to share that with her. She surrendered control, focused once again on her own happiness, went back to participating in the activities that she enjoyed, and within six months met a wonderful man who loves her as much as she loves him. She finally surrendered to her heart rather than her mind's projection of the heart's desire.

- I realized several years into my engineering career that designing avionics systems was not what I wanted to do for the rest of my life. My mind went crazy trying to figure out what I could do instead. I agonized for months, made a fool of myself applying for jobs that didn't suit me and finally gave up. I surrendered to the fact that all I knew was that I wanted to wake up happy, go to bed grateful, help people, and make a decent living. Thus began a series of events that rearranged my entire life. I could not have planned the inception of my current career had I tried. I had to surrender my mind's projections of what I *thought* would make an ideal career in order to be guided into one I truly loved.

- At another point in my life, I wanted a house. I

did what I knew to do. I drove around and looked at houses. I found one I loved except for the fact that it cost several thousand dollars more than I could afford to spend. Furthermore, it was missing a bathtub in the bathroom. In spite of its shortcomings, my mind was certain that this was the home for me because it was the closest thing I'd seen to the house of my dreams. Had I been able to afford it, I would have settled for a house that required major bathroom renovations.

Happily, the River was carrying me towards something better. At this almost-dream home, I met a Realtor who "adopted" me. I explained my needs and two days later, after I gave up looking altogether, he sent me several property listings. One stood out among the rest. I went to see this house after a client "coincidentally" cancelled her appointment the following day. I walked in the front door and immediately knew this would be my home. There was no struggle and no effort. I made an offer that was accepted two hours later.

I could have resisted myself and agonized over the more expensive home. I could have given up, thinking that the universe was never going to give me something affordable. I could have bought the more expensive home and put myself into debt, settling for something that wasn't right. However, in this case, the River helped me surrender to what my heart really wanted – a great home that was also affordable and had *all* the elements I desired.

I took the action that I knew to take. When no other options were apparent, I waited for the next step to be revealed. Finally, I listened to the strong urge to see the house that is now mine.

As you can see there are times to float on the River and take time in stillness, and then there are times to paddle, or take action in your life. If you learn when to be still versus when to take action, your life will flow with incredible grace.

I have come up with a simple guideline that works very well in my own life:

I never take action towards a goal unless I am very clear on the goal and inspired to take a specific action. If both of those conditions are not met, I create time in silence and solitude each day, sometimes five minutes or less, to get clear and wait in stillness to see if any thoughts or inspirations about what to do next arise. If none do, I simply enjoy my regular activities, trusting that when the time is right, the ideas and inspiration will find me.

Waiting for the River to inform you before taking action is one of life's greatest secrets to happiness. To summarize the process of navigating the River:

1. Take time in stillness to get in touch with your own heart.

2. Take the actions that you know to do, to support your heart's goals.

3. When you haven't a clue or an inspiration on what to do next, wait! Do nothing. Pray and spend time in stillness waiting for the answer. Enjoy your life.

4. When you get the urge or inspiration to take action, do so. Then wait for guidance once again, repeat the process with faith, and trust that the River is carrying you towards your true heart's desires.

The process of surrendering to the River takes practice, patience, faith, and a surrendering of control. Nevertheless, learning these skills will bring you a life of grace and ease – one without undue effort and struggle. Learning when to paddle and when to float will help free up your time and energy for more enjoyable pursuits and help you fill your proverbial cup so you are healthy, rested, happy, and on the path to your dreams.

VI. Boulders & Blockages

There are times when you feel you are doing everything right in the outside world and yet life is still not working. You're listening to the voices in your heart. You've surrendered control. You've been patient. You've done what you feel guided to do, and yet your dreams are nowhere in sight. Worse yet, you seem to be attracting the same mess time and again. Consider these all-too-common examples:

- You know you deserve a healthy relationship, and yet you attract the same type of dysfunctional partner time and again.

- As soon as you begin to feel in control of your finances, some unforeseen expense sends you back into debt.

- You feel as if the minute you start doing something for yourself, someone you love has a greater need for your time.

- You resolve to find a new career, start a new hobby, take time for yourself, exercise, eat better, etc., but you always find an excuse not to do these things.

- You want to do something but feel too stupid, broke, exhausted, etc., to begin.

This could be a very long list if I enumerated the myriad of examples I have witnessed in my own life and the lives of my clients. We all have times when, when in spite of our best intentions, some unknown force inside of us seems to keep sabotaging our dreams and intentions.

It's easy to blame the outside world. Its easy to pretend you're the victim of the individuals you've dated, the car that broke down right before your bills were due, and the parents who never validated you and let you know you were smart, beautiful, and pure inside. You're human. We all slip into blame at times.

However, the reality of life on earth is that there are hurtful people, products that aren't built well, and parents who are hurt children themselves. There are perpetrators, greedy corporations, swindlers, cons, and a variety of people and things that can get us down. The question to ponder is, "Why do we attract some of these situations and people into our lives repeatedly when there are also wonderful people, great businesses, and helpful souls?"

The answer will not be found in the outer world, but rather deep within our own hearts and minds. The River wants to course through our lives in a graceful and kind manner. Through past pains and traumas, judgments against others and ourselves, and unhealthy habits, attitudes, or beliefs, we create boulders and blockages that divert its natural course.

We need to dive deep within ourselves and be honest about where we block the flow of God's Love and grace in our lives. If a river runs into a bed of rock, it takes a divergent course. So too, when God's Love runs into a blockage, it will do its best to steer you into situations, circumstances, and relationships where you can see and release this block. Then the River can once again guide you with ease. God is not cruel. God wants to love us and pour love into our lives. Grace will work gently at first to reveal our blockages then more strongly, if required, to get our attention.

Look at pure and innocent children, and you will witness the River flowing quite freely through these tiny beings. Children love easily, express freely, and move about life without fear. Now consider yourself. Can you love easily, express freely, and move through life without undue fear? Chances are that in some areas of your life you can, and in others, you feel blocked. You may know conceptually that you can create anything you want, yet something continues to stop you.

There are entire books written about how we develop these unconscious patterns and beliefs. In this book, I am more concerned with how we free ourselves from these blockages. Allow me to share a few examples:

- Temporary blockages occur all too frequently. A woman chooses to sleep an extra twenty minutes which feels absolutely wonderful, but when she finally gets out of bed she starts berating herself and telling herself she will have to rush to run her errands. She hurries through her morning routine, stubs her toe, spills her coffee, cleans up the mess, hurries to get in the car and after driving down the road realizes that she forgot the bills that she needs to drop in the mail. She goes back home, unlocks the house, and rushes through her day feeling frazzled. She appears to attract every angry driver in traffic. When she finally slows down, she realizes that sleeping late was not the culprit. Berating herself created a lack of focus that contributed to her crazy day.

- Deeper patterns can cause more pain. A man loves his family and children but seems to be under constant financial stress. He handles the pressure fairly well, but today he receives his bank statement that shows that he forgot to deduct a bill from his checking account. It was an honest mistake, but he learned early in life to be "perfect," and he berates himself without mercy. As a result, he is short tempered with his family and children who choose to go to the movies without him. He feels abandoned and thinks he deserves this. Only in time, after having deep conversations with his wife and children, does he discover that they don't judge him nearly as harshly as he judges himself, and they truly would *want* to be with him if he were kinder.

Ingrained patterns and blockages can wreak havoc in our lives. Suppose you have a million things to do but you just want some comfort. You want to call a friend, watch a movie, or put your feet up and have a cup of tea, but you feel as if life won't support you if you take this time off to relax. As you repeatedly ignore your heart, you become tired, needy, and irritable.

If you're single, you begin to fantasize that a partner will come into your life and make it all better. He or she will give you money, cook for you, or make your life happier in ways you are not choosing to make your life happier. The fantasies get bigger, until you meet someone who likes you, flatters you, and makes you feel wonderful. The fantasy seems real! This is the one! Then reality hits. Weeks or months down the road, you realize your partner is human too, has needs, insecurities, fears, and patterns just like you. He or she is not going to rescue you after all. What happens next is entirely up to you. You can admit that you created the situation and seek counseling in order to grow closer or bow out with dignity. In less attractive scenarios, you get angry and try to change, manipulate, or bully the other into being the fantasy you were seeking, or worse yet, you beat yourself up. These strategies never work.

If you're already in a relationship and you're not taking care of yourself, the "fight or flight" syndrome usually kicks in. Most people will either begin to withdraw, feeling they cannot be with another and take care of their own needs, or they'll become angry and irritable with their partner and blame him or her for the problems. When these patterns occur, ask yourself who told you that you couldn't take care of yourself in a partnership? If it's your partner, get help or leave with grace. Most often, it is a pattern or belief in your own mind.

If your life is not working and patterns seem to keep repeating in spite of your best intentions, or you feel stuck in spite of doing everything right, here are a few tried and true suggestions for removing blockages:

GET REAL AND GET RID OF THE NEED TO PLEASE:

You have to be honest with yourself about your feelings and desires if you are going to get unstuck. Take inventory of your life. Where are you not admitting to God and the world around you that you want change? Admitting that we want change can be terrifying. This level of honesty can mean you have to tell a partner that some aspect of the relationship isn't working, or admit that despite the fact that your parents paid for your engineering college education that you want to pursue a new career talking to angels!

Getting real can be hard work. Getting real might mean admitting you want something in life that you have been told is "too much to ask," something you "shouldn't" want, or something "irresponsible." Responses from loved ones can vary from kind and supportive to a lot less. "Are you crazy?" "How do you think you'll do that?" "Why are you always complaining? Can't you be satisfied with what you have?"

Do not let the world tell you who you should be and how you should feel.

Trying to please others is the number one blockage to the River's flow through your own heart and mind. We learned that we would be loved conditionally because human beings love that way, and yet we must break past that illusion. Pray with all your heart to know God's unconditional love. God put those crazy dreams in your heart so you would honor them, grow, learn, and be all that you were designed to be. If you study famous people who are making a huge difference in the world, you will learn that at some point they had to stop pleasing others and learn to march to the beat of their own drum.

The disease to please is a huge blockage to the River. My friends and I now joke, "Please don't *should* on me!" It is human to want others to love you, but if you get real and choose to be yourself without shame, you will attract the people who belong in your life and lose the ones who don't. God can handle that. Just be you. Get help if you need it from books, counselors, coaches, healers, religion, spirituality, or any other healthy avenue. Do what it takes to strengthen your resolve to be yourself. This is what the River wants from you. This is what the River wants for you.

DIVE DEEP AND FIND THE FEARS:

Do the breathing exercises from Chapter 2. If you find blockages, there are many ways to heal them. You can learn a form of energetic healing such as Reiki, which is readily available in most locations. You can visit a healer. You can choose a discipline such as yoga or tai chi, which moves and unblocks the body's energies. You can breathe deeply into the stuck spot and imagine the energy flowing there until you begin to feel an emotion. Next, allow the tears to flow, or the anger to surface, until you discover a deeper truth.

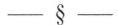

Breathing Through the Blockages

Sit or lay comfortably where you will not be interrupted for a few minutes. Focus on your breath. Don't change it or try to breathe more deeply. Imagine that the breath goes throughout your entire body. Scan your body and see where there are tight spots that seem to block the natural flow of energy.

Pick one of these tight or uncomfortable spaces to focus on. Breathe as if you can breathe right into that spot. Imagine the air enters your lungs, and then becomes energy that travels into that spot. As you exhale, imagine tension leaving that spot.

If this is a minor blockage, the breathing may release all the tension. If not, keep breathing, slowly. Don't hyperventilate. Feel the resistance to the energy and the love. Feel the area's resistance to the River of God's Love. Stay with this feeling even though it might be uncomfortable. If you become emotional, feel the feelings but don't analyze them. Just let them flow. They need to be released, that is all.

If nothing is coming up and there is no sense of release, mentally ask the tight spot, "Who is in there and what do you need?" Memories are stuck in the body. See what comes up for you and imagine you can send love, healing, and nurturing to whatever presents itself in your imagination. Let go. Be very sweet to yourself. This is deep work.

— § —

If the exercise is too difficult or if you feel you've had a traumatic past, it would be best to do this with the help of a licensed therapist or certified hypnotherapist. These people are trained to help you move through the possibly unpleasant emotions that may arise. Don't let that make you shy away from healing. "Better out than in," the angels always say about our past traumas. There is no need to store the pains you've already healed in your body. There is no need to continue to suffer. Help is available in many forms these days. When you are confused, pray. God will always guide you to help that is right for you.

Two years have passed since I broke my foot. It is completely healed now and I feel much more balanced in my life. I can honestly tell friends when I need "down time." I have wonderful people in my life. I have time to do my private sessions, teach classes, maintain a website, house, business, two dogs, and numerous friendships. Somehow, it all works since I lost the desire to "make nice" and please everyone. I found my spirit again. Miraculously the River keeps running through me onto these pages.

I recently realized that a huge energetic blockage in my throat and jaws was coming to the surface. It manifested first as stuck energy that I noticed in meditations, and then it turned into tightness and pain. I did all my usual tricks. I got real and had some conversations I needed to have. I took inventory of sadness and anger and resolved them, but when the pain didn't quit, I prayed for help. "God help me release whatever is causing this pain."

A friend who happens to be a phenomenal healer himself[6] (the same one that "helped" me break my foot!) recommended a chiropractor[7] who is one of the most amazing shaman/healers I've ever met. He'd never call himself that, but I do. He works on my energy as well as my spine and doesn't say too much during our sessions. Nonetheless, the River

---

[6] James Walker, www.meditation4peace.com, chi massage, tai chi instruction, healing, meditation classes, etc.

[7] Dr. Shawn K. Warwick, Touch for Life, (480) 429-9433

directs him and he quickly managed to get flow going in my energy field around the throat. After one particularly powerful session, he looked at me with such huge compassion and I almost laughed. I knew *that* look. I give *that* look to people after some of my healing sessions. That look said, "We just pulled a cork and you're going to have some heavy duty emotional release." Two days later, I was bawling my eyes out in front of two of my cherished friends after realizing I was terrified of losing the people I loved if I was going to write books, speak my truth more publicly, and risk bringing more of myself to the surface in front of the world.

The blockage was created by real events in my life and the fears that ensued inside of me. Almost every time I've made a major life change, people I cherished not only left me but also did so with anger and judgment. I lost a dear childhood girlfriend to her religious zealousness when I began my career as an angel communicator. She wrote me a letter to cast out my "demons" and may never understand that I too love God as much as she does. After breaking up kindly with a guy I was casually dating because he demanded too much attention for himself and was unwilling to help others in need, he sought me out the next day in a public place and lambasted me in front of a crowd of co-workers. When I left engineering to pursue my dreams, someone I thought was a good friend called me up to yell at me. "How *dare* you leave me?" she cried, never realizing the friendship could have continued. I've had hate mail sent to me by those who don't understand me because I talk to angels. I've been judged by the classrooms in which I teach. I've had people who were later diagnosed with borderline personality disorder yell at me and ask me, "how on earth I could consider myself spiritual" when I refused to become their personal savior.

This fear of being attacked lay patiently dormant inside of me until I committed to writing my books, speaking out in public more, and asking for more in my life. Then the ghosts of my past began to rise up and haunt me. I was terrified of people's angry responses to my healthy choices. I had an inner belief that said, "don't change or you'll be persecuted." I had locked tears of terror in my throat and jaws. God answered my prayers in the form of a shaman/healer to work on my energy, two friends to love me through it, and two hours of sobbing my eyes out. The block is gone. I'm able to write this chapter and complete this book at long last.

FORGIVE & RELEASE THE ANGER:

Unforgiveness is another huge blockage to the flow of grace in your life. The angels often say, "You may have been victimized but it is your choice to remain a victim." We choose not to forgive for a variety of reasons, but the bottom line is that we don't want to give persecutors the impression that whatever they did was okay, and we want to protect ourselves from future pain. Both of these reasons for holding on to unforgiveness, however, actually hurt *us*, not the perpetrator.

Forgiveness is not saying that what was done to you is ok. Forgiveness is not saying, "I give you

permission to hurt me again or to hurt others."
Forgiveness is not feeling warm and fuzzy about the
ones who hurt you, nor does it demand that you
should accept them back in your life. Forgiveness
does not even have to include a conversation with
the one who caused you pain. Forgiveness is an act
of grace. It is a gift you give yourself to release
yourself from a painful past. Forgiveness is saying,
"I no longer give the past power over my future!"
Forgiveness is saying, "You hurt me, but I release
the effects of your words and actions. Go your way
and I give myself the freedom to go mine."

As long as you hold on to unforgiveness, you
remain chained – energetically and emotionally – to
the one that hurt you. Furthermore, in
unforgiveness, we continue to remain a victim in
our own minds, and we attract the same repeatedly
until we learn that it is our choice to decide not to
remain a victim.

Forgiveness is a courageous act of taking
responsibility for your future instead of blaming
your past. When I forgave the ex-boyfriend who

owed me money, blessed him, and released him, my abundance returned. My forgiveness had little to do with him. It was a gift of freedom I gave to myself.

When you forgive, you take back responsibility for your future. You release the past, learn from it, and move on. When you forgive, you cut the ties that bind you. Forgiveness really has nothing to do with the other. Once again, *forgiveness is a gift you give yourself.*

PRAY:

I am a firm believer that God wants to help us. If you feel stuck in an area of your life, pray for God to reveal and help you release any blockages to having what you want. Then get ready to release control. Your prayers will be answered. Pay attention to the subtle signals, and trust that everything that follows in your life is an answer to this prayer. God does listen. Always.

VII. Waterfalls & Unforeseen Turns

The River has a mind of its own. It will always guide you to a life better than you've planned, but a huge degree of faith and trust in God's goodness is required in order to surrender to its powerful flow. I used to insist on doing things the hard way in my life. I swam instead of sailing. I tried to control situations and people in order to mold them to my liking. Now I surrender to what comes, change what I can, and allow the rest to simply be. I trust that somehow God has my good at heart, no matter what happens in my life. I still throw the occasional tantrum but I get over it quickly, pick myself up, dust off, and move forward. God knows what He's doing.

I recently put my car in the shop for some major repairs. The expense was formidable at this point in my life, but I refuse to bother worrying about money because God always pays my bills. I have more important things to focus on. When I drove the car away from the shop, I heard a terrible clunking noise in the back. Frightened and a bit irritated I drove back to the shop and asked the mechanic to see what was going on. I knew I was going to be late for an appointment because of this inconvenience, but there was nothing I could do so I surrendered.

The wonderful young woman who had worked on my car came out front to investigate the noise. She discovered it was simply a loose jack that needed to be fastened in the trunk. However, she was very glad I had returned to the shop. She had left a message for me with the service advisor who managed my car, but he had called in sick and so I had not received the message. The timing belt was very loose, she said, and could break at any moment. She suggested I get it fixed as soon as possible. I put my car back in the shop, got a new rental car, and was late for my appointment. Nonetheless, my original frustration gave way to huge gratitude. What looked like an annoyance ended up being a life– or at least timesaving stroke of grace. My car could have broken down on a long stretch of highway that I frequently drive. Instead I was simply fifteen minutes late for an appointment and my car works perfectly now. Many times in my life, a minor annoyance has kept me off the freeway for a few minutes, and as a result, I've narrowly missed several major accidents.

There are times when it seems as if God must be crazy. We pray for peace and are thrust into chaos that redirects our life. We pray for an increase in salary and are laid off. We pray for abundance and our income slows down enough for us to take time, reassess our life, and start a new career. I prayed for balance and broke my foot!

When life throws you into unforeseen and unexpected circumstances, you've gone over a waterfall in the River. If you can suspend judgment and embrace change, these unforeseen circumstances may turn out to be the biggest gifts heaven has bestowed upon you. Consider these real-life examples:

- A delightful man I met went over the falls when he was laid off three times in a row by large corporations that were "down-sizing." He had a fantastic attitude and figured that God must have other plans. He told me that he loved his dog and he loved photography. "My dog Vinny," he told me, "has a natural talent for rock climbing." This beautiful man started taking pictures of his dog wearing climbing gear. Vinny is now featured in several climbing magazines[8] and on screensavers sold to large corporations. His owner plans to include his entire family in the business and has a knack for uplifting and inspiring everyone he meets.

- My own mother developed thyroid cancer. During the course of her healing, she decided to truly live her life instead of simply existing to serve others. She learned to speak up instead of stuffing her feelings and has emerged as a wise woman who now provides great light in the lives of others. She is more empowered

---

[8] http://vinnythepug.photosite.com/

than ever before.

• Due to unforeseen expenses, a woman I know was forced to close her retail store, move to a smaller house and stay at home for awhile. During this "mandatory down time," as the angels called it, she discovered her artistic talents and a huge sense of self-worth. As a result, she now makes beautiful and empowering healing dolls that charm and delight all who see them.

• Three clients of mine all went over the same waterfall in their individual lives when their seemingly perfect marriages fell apart and they discovered their husband's secret addictions. In each case, with uncanny similarity, the women had been very loving to spouses who were less than kind to them. The experience of "going over the falls" freed these women from their secret bondage to unloving partners. One woman is enjoying her newfound self-esteem immensely. Another has found the love of her life. The third has overcome tremendous fears to find an incredible inner peace. In each case, the River brought them closer to God and their own hearts.

- A man I know is a very giving angel in his relationships and business dealings. He gave and gave to those who took and took from him. A breakdown helped him find his own sweet heart and realize his inner worth. After recuperating from his trip over the waterfall, he has discovered a kinder business and gentler relationships.

- I have been over the falls numerous times in my life – through divorce, being dumped by a boyfriend who owed me money, breaking my foot, etc. In each case, God had better plans for me than the circumstances that I was willing to settle for in my own life.

At times, an unforeseen change is the only way that God can get you into a better situation. What seems to be a disaster is almost certainly a blessing in disguise. We have to reserve judgment when life comes with surprises. Quite likely God is bringing you a better life, more faith and trust, new gifts and abilities, more open and loving relationships, greater balance, and healthier self-esteem. You don't know the end of the story during the first scene of a movie. You have to wait to see how God's plan unfolds in your life.

I keep my favorite quote on my desk at all times:

> *We must be willing to get rid of the life we've planned so as to have the life that is waiting for us. – Joseph Campbell*[9]

When you go over the waterfall, it does not necessarily mean you have done anything wrong. It simply means that God had to resort to drastic measures to bring change into your life. If possible, God brings changes gently and kindly. Joy calls to your soul first. "Try a new career. Rest more. Speak up in your relationship." Listen to these subtle urges, and you will grow and move with the

River more easily.

If we ignore the quiet signals, life becomes a little more difficult. Your current job becomes increasingly unsatisfactory. You develop physical discomfort. Your spouse becomes more distant. The River is giving you not-so-subtle signs that something needs to change in your life, even if that means having an honest conversation, taking time in stillness, or admitting you want more in silent prayer.

If you don't heed the kinder messages or the more challenging ones, you will almost certainly end up going over the waterfall as I did. Life will suddenly catapult you into a situation where you must grow up, speak up, make changes, or leave an unhealthy situation. You are fired. You develop disease. Your spouse leaves you. A disaster strikes. These life-shattering, earth-shaking changes necessitate a different way of being.

When life throws you into unexpected

---

[9] Campbell, Joseph. *Joseph Campbell Companion, A*: Reflections on the Art of Living:

circumstances, the only way to navigate the River gracefully is to embrace what has occurred, grieve if you must, get in touch with your heart, ask God to reveal the next step, and take action when guided. The sooner we get back to sailing, the more quickly joy returns. Here are my tried-and-true steps for moving forward after "going over the waterfall."

1.   ACCEPT WHAT HAS OCCURRED.

What good does it do to wish something hadn't happened when it is done? The past is the past, and no amount of wishful thinking, wondering what you could have done differently, or berating your choices will change that.

Change what you can by all means, and accept what you can't change. There is no point to resisting what has already occurred in your life. Wail, scream, kick, cry, and get the tantrums out of your system. I have had some rip-roaring rants in my life before I calmed down enough to realize that God was wreaking havoc in my life to help get me

New York, NY: Harper's Trade, 1995.

unstuck.

Even if you've been victimized, choose to stop labeling yourself a victim. Whatever happened already happened. You cannot change the past. However, you *can* focus on the future you want to create. Stop, slow down, and accept your own feelings as well.

Waterfalls are designed to propel you into the depths of your own heart so you can bring your truth up to the surface once again.

2.   IF YOU NEED TO GRIEVE, GRIEVE.

We are human and sadness is simply our soul's method of releasing wishful thinking so we can accept what is. If we could truly live each moment, one moment at a time, we would not grieve so deeply. However, it is human nature to project expectations into the future. When these hopes are dashed, we grieve. We are releasing imagined futures and getting back into the present. This is not easy. I cried at my grandmother's funeral even though I saw her smiling and waving at me in spirit. I wailed each night for seven months after my divorce, feeling like a failure until at long last I realized I was not. Give in to your feelings; let them run their course. Time heals.

You're human. It's ok.

Get counseling if you have gone through death of a loved one, have health issues, or have suffered from abuse or trauma. Find support groups. Pray and ask others to pray for you. Ask friends honestly and directly for comfort. Denial doesn't work. Addictions don't work. Trying to manipulate other people into loving us by incessantly repeating our sob stories only alienates friends.

Instead, be kind to yourself and ask friends for comfort honestly and directly. Most people want to help others and will do so kindly if you ask for the help without manipulation. "I need a shoulder to cry on. Do you have a few minutes to talk?" is a statement that will be much more readily received with love and kindness than an endless litany of "poor me."

3. ASK YOURSELF WHAT YOU DESIRE NEXT.

Try to focus on what you want next in your life, not what you wish would have or should have happened, but what you want in the very next breath. It is difficult to maintain this focus. We tend to want to go back and change the past, but we can't. If you lose a loved one, you can't change that, but you can admit that you need comfort and someone to hold your hand while you cry. If you lose a job, you may want another one similar to the first, or an entirely new career. If a spouse leaves you, you want comfort and perhaps a kinder relationship. Forget about wanting revenge. The point of this step is to ask what you want and need for yourself, not the other.

This can be an incredible time of soul searching and self-discovery if you embrace the process. You can use the unforeseen circumstance as an excuse to reassess and recreate your life. Is it time to give up on something that isn't working? Is it time to start something new? Is it time to admit a feeling you've been pushing aside? Find the answer in your heart.

4. ASK GOD TO REVEAL THE NEXT STEP IN YOUR LIFE AND WAIT UNTIL YOU GET THE URGE TO DO SOMETHING.

Don't be stoic and force yourself to act when you need rest and comfort. Ask for more assistance than you usually would from friends, community, church, or family. Get over any pride that gets in the way and realize that as much as you give, there are times to receive as well.

5. TRUST THAT GOD LOVES YOU AND THERE WILL BE GOOD THAT COMES OUT OF THE SITUATION IF YOU DO YOUR PART AND EMBRACE THE CHANGE.

This is so much more easily said than done. The only way I know to trust is to make the choice to think thoughts aligned with faith. We can't control our feelings, but we can choose our thoughts and control our actions. I have an overactive mind. That comes in handy when I'm writing a book, preparing for a class, or researching a topic. However, when I start overanalyzing my life, it drives me crazy. I actually say to my thoughts, "Stop! Accept life as it is! Trust in God's Love." I have a sign on my refrigerator that says, "Trust in God's great love for you." I can choose my perspective. I can say "no" to negative self-defeating thoughts. So can you. It just takes practice and developing a little mental muscle. Think of this as an exercise program for your soul.

We tend to overanalyze traumatic changes because we think that by understanding them we can outsmart God in the future. That's impossible. However, you can reflect honestly and see if you were ignoring your own heart before going over the waterfall. You can learn from this introspection.

When I broke my foot, it was not difficult for me to see that I had been ignoring my need for balance even when I prayed for the same. However there have been other times when I really didn't understand why I ended up going into the rapids (chaotic times in life) or over the falls (unforeseen circumstances). During those times, I pray for insight.

A few months ago, I felt as if I was on top of the world. The following week everything that could break in my home decided to break including my air conditioner, vacuum, pool pump, etc. The repairs created financial challenges and complicated my schedule. I didn't have a clue what I had done to attract the mess, so I laid in bed one morning praying for insight. Two minutes later, the clock radio came on playing a song with the lyrics "Something's got to go wrong 'cause I'm feeling way too damn good."[10] In a moment of honesty, I laughed hysterically. I realized that I had indeed harbored a fear that every time life went well, something would happen to mess it up. The River brought this subconscious belief right up to the surface of my life.

When thieves broke into my old car, shattered the window, caused a huge mess, and stole the radio, I remember thinking to myself, "Well better me than someone else. I can handle it." I asked the angels why I attracted the burglary. "This time," they

---

[10] Nickelback, *"Feelin' Way Too Damn Good"* from *The Long Road.* Roadrunner Records, 2003.

informed me, I didn't exactly "attract" it, but rather "allowed" for it. At that time in my life, I had no healthy boundaries, and life mirrored this. As always, the angels reminded me to simply learn from the experience rather than beat myself up or remain a victim. "Learn and move on," they advised me.

Life occurs in cycles. We go through death and rebirth many times throughout the course of our lives. Sometimes we have to release a part of life, a situation, or a person, in order to grow and make room for more joy in our lives. These are not easy times, yet have faith that new life always follows death. Spring will eternally follow winter.

If you are too exhausted to move on after going over one of life's waterfalls, rest. Cocoon yourself. The River will always bring you back to life in its own time. Relief always follows tears. New career opportunities appear after old jobs expire. Love blossoms no matter how much pain you've experienced. Your life will go on no matter what has happened. If you are on a raft on the River, you are still moving.

It is the very movement of God that will carry you forward.

Give thanks for the times when you have gone over the waterfall. Stop struggling against what has occurred and be still. The River will bring you back up to the surface and help you move on with your life. Trust that beneath all of life's ups and downs, the deeper currents of God's Love are always at work. Reserve judgment and wait for the miracles that await you downstream.

VIII.   The Destination is Love

The River has one and only one destination and that is to bring you to an awareness of the fact that you are part of God's loving creation here upon the earth. You matter to God. You are a cell in His body, a part of His unfolding plan to allow you to experience and expand His love. You are an integral part of the whole. If your life works, you contribute to the lives of others with joy and ease. You may exert effort, but you won't struggle. You may go through challenging times, but like the Phoenix arising from its own ashes, you will be reborn with greater understanding, ability, and inspiration. If you embrace the currents of the River, you will find you are very, very loved.

When I began writing this book over two years ago, the River took over my life. The book flowed as God willed it, not as I dictated. The book was written by my life, and my life was written by this book.

The first time I wrote the first chapter there was too much intellect and too little heart. God took over and my computer trashed the file somehow. I had to start from scratch. Love wins. The River kept flowing through my life whether I cooperated with God's Love or fought it.

To navigate the River of God's Love you truly have to trust that it has an inherent intelligence and plan for your life – a plan that calls for a life better than one you could create on your own. The River of God's Love knows things you can't even imagine. If you allow yourself to be carried by its currents, Divine grace will guide your life.

Navigating the River means we have to unlearn so much of what we have taken as truth throughout human existence. We have to let go of trying to control our future. We have to take time in stillness and reconnect with our heart's true desires. We have to act on those subtle, positive whispers in our heart. We have to speak up even when we know the conversations will be difficult, and we must remain committed to being impeccably honest with ourselves.

We have to take time to notice the signals in our body and be aware when the energy is blocked. If you practice the energy-sensing exercises outlined in this book, you can learn to detect and correct energetic blockages before they manifest in illness. You can learn to pay attention to the gentle currents of the River before you go over the waterfalls. You can pray to have boulders and blockages removed so you can continue on the most graceful course in life.

God is always trying to help you in your life. God wants you to express the wonder and glory of His creation, which includes you. You are part of God's creation and if you are living an authentic, inspired, self-expressed existence, you pay tribute to God's great love. You allow the creator to guide creation into its most amazing form. You surrender to Love.

I never know where the River will take me. Even on those days when I jump in with abandon and grace, trusting in the safe flow, I could be tossed into the rapids. I have to live with that. I have to embrace the chaos, the certain uncertainty, and the predictable unpredictability of life. If I can surrender to that, all is bliss. Anything less is struggle, pain and disappointment. In the words of one of my greatest teachers and friends, "Expect nothing and appreciate everything."[11] Love is the River of life. Surrender. The currents of grace long to carry you safely into the ocean of God's great all-embracing love.

---

[11] Zeysan, *Table of Ancients*. Victoria B.C.: Canada, 2002.
www.templeofthetwindragons.com

IX. Epilogue

I had no sooner finished the last chapter of this book, when an incoming email captured my attention. The subject line read "Great Day at the Falls." My jaw dropped. The email was from my father.

As I stared incredulously at the computer, the River rushed through me with such intensity, I felt as if I were on fire. Heat coursed through my body, up my spine, and then out through my hands and feet. My entire being vibrated. I surrendered and felt the bliss of heaven telling me, "Job well done, dear Ann. Job well done." This book has taken me over two years to write and caused more growth than any other project I've undertaken.

There, in my father's email was a photograph of the waterfall from my childhood where the entire journey began. The falls have become shallower over the years. The rocks have been moved around by the River as it changes course and form, but nonetheless the River continues to flow into eternity. So do we.

My father said both he and my mom had awakened with the same idea to visit those falls today. They live three thousand miles away from me. They did not know I was working on my book, and furthermore, they didn't even know that I even mentioned the falls in this book.

What motivated my parents to visit those falls today – on the day I finished this book? None other than the River of God's Love that works unceasingly in our lives to guide, validate, amaze, and surprise us. Trust the River. Trust in God's Love for you. It will eternally be there.

Love is the River

May you leap into your heart, and surrender to a Divine flow of grace that will lead you to life beyond your wildest dreams!

About the Author

Ann Albers graduated from the University of Notre Dame in 1986 with a Bachelor's degree in Electrical Engineering then worked in the avionics industry for 8 years before leaving to pursue her spiritual calling

She is now a popular Author, Angel Communicator, Spiritual Instructor, and Modern Mystic whose life is dedicated to helping others discover the power and beauty of their souls, and a deep, joyful connection with the Divine.

Most recently Ann became a conduit for a pure loving energy that seems to catalyze transformation, and even miracles for many.

It is her great delight to help you create a joyful and loving experience of heaven here on earth!

If you liked this book...

Visit Ann's website

www.visionsofheaven.com

Subscribe to our free weekly newsletter:

"Messages from Ann & the Angels"

Enjoy Other Books by Ann:

Whispers of the Spirit

Bridging the Gap Between Christianity & Mysticism

And So Much More...

Free Articles, Online Programs, Live Classes,

Classes on CD | MP3, Angel Meditations,

Recipes, the Angel Playroom, and more...

See Love • Be Love

Made in the USA
Las Vegas, NV
02 June 2022

49682065R00114